THE ETIQUETTE
OF ILLNESS

THE ETIQUETTE OF ILLNESS

What to Say When You Can't Find the Words

Susan P. Halpern

BLOOMSBURY PRESS

NEW YORK • LONDON • NEW DELHI • SYDNEY

Published by Bloomsbury USA, New York

All papers used by Bloomsbury are natural, recyclable
products made from wood grown in well-managed forests.
The manufacturing processes conform to the environmental
regulations of the country of origin.

Library of Congress Cataloging-in-Publication Data
Halpern, Susan P.
The etiquette of illness: what to say when you can't find the words / Susan
P. Halpern.—1st U.S. ed.
p. cm.
ISBN 1-58234-383-7
ISBN-13 978-1-58234-383-9
1. Medicine and psychology—Miscellanea. 2. Sick—Psychology—
Miscellanea. 3. Interpersonal communication—Miscellanea. l. Title.
R726.5.H327 2004
616'.001'9—dc22
2003022604

First U.S. Edition 2004

5 7 9 10 8 6

Typeset by Hewer Text Ltd, Edinburgh
Printed in the United States by Thomson-Shore, Inc. Dexter, Michigan

This book is dedicated to Charles, with love

Contents

Preface

My friend Paul Gorman called at nine-thirty on a Saturday morning and asked me earnestly, "Do you want me to ask you about the CAT scan you had this week? I don't know if you want to talk about it."

I was delighted by Paul's question and could not wait to answer him. And I was also struck by the form of his question. For me, Paul's formulation in seeking information was respectful and caring, and opened the way to a long conversation. He wanted to know how I was. He wanted to know how I would be. He wanted to know how I had reacted to what was on my plate. But he also did not want me to have to talk about my scan if I wasn't ready or in the mood. In his question I heard that he cared about my need for privacy, and that he wanted to support my husband and me with his friendship. By asking the question, "Do you want me to ask," he was able both to ask for information and give me the space I needed.

I replied, "If you are a good enough friend to know that I had a CAT scan this week, you are a good enough friend to ask how it went." I was touched that Paul remembered and that he wanted to know the results. By putting his interest forward in the form of a particular kind of question, he gave me the right to answer him as I needed to. We went on to talk about the difficulties of addressing friends, family, and strangers about illness or death.

Can there be an etiquette book for this subject? Is there a right way? How do we make ourselves more comfortable talking about illness? We tossed these questions back and forth. I was intrigued. This topic felt important to me. I have been fumbling my way through sympathy cards and condolences all my life, and now because of a cancer diagnosis I am often on the receiving end.

There *should* be a book, I thought. To write about this subject would give me the opportunity to tell the stories of the people in the support groups I have been facilitating for six years, as well as stories from my own life and the lives of my friends. So many people with insight and courage have shared their stories with me during my journey with cancer. Now I finally have a chance to tell their stories and to help others find their way to a comfortable exchange of words.

MY STORY

In 1995, I was diagnosed with low-grade lymphoma, a cancer of the immune system. Since then, I have been working with individuals and leading groups to support people with cancer. I had spent sixteen years as a psychotherapist working with individuals, families, and groups, and then taken time out from my practice in the late '80s and '90s to cofound a nonprofit organization committed to developing permanent housing for people who were homeless and mentally ill in New York City. The satisfaction of seeing brand new efficiency apartments grow out of the discarded housing stock of the City of New York, watching communities improve, and then witnessing the delight of the tenants selected to move into the completely renovated dwellings was enormous. After my diagnosis, however, I began to dream of sitting quietly in an office and listening to people sort through their lives when faced with difficult medical situations. I wanted to practice psychotherapy again. Two of my friends, Ram Dass and Joan Halifax, were offering support to people who were dying, and they talked about the satisfaction they were finding in that work. They spoke of the possibility of people having a "good death" and what that was like for both the person and caregiver. The lack of adequate care for people and their families at the end of life was beginning to receive attention, and I wanted to be part of the growing group of people serving in this field.

In December of 1995 I participated in a program in Bolinas, California, for people with cancer, called the Commonweal Cancer Help Program. I had first heard of Commonweal from a friend who was one of its first participants, and later I met Michael Lerner, one of the cofounders of Commonweal. Commonweal was featured on the Bill Moyers PBS special *Healing and the Mind* in 1989. By the time I was diagnosed, Michael was a friend, and I remember well the night he called, as we were choosing oncologists. He called to offer my husband and me his expertise and concern for what had entered our lives and, as he knew, would change them forever. Not long after that I went to

Michael's weeklong program for people with cancer. The purpose of the week is to explore of what cancer means for each of the eight participants. It is a time to learn experientially what it takes to heal and to begin to make choices for what kinds of care and treatment will offer each participant the best chance at living fully for as long as possible after leaving the retreat. During that week I began to speak aloud about my dream of leaving my job to work with people with cancer. With the support of the Commonweal experience, I was able to move in the direction I had dreamed of going.

The next spring, as I was getting ready to leave the housing program and go on sabbatical in Italy for three months with my husband, Michael Lerner called to say he was starting an East Coast program that would replicate the Commonweal Cancer Help Program. He hoped that I would consider joining the staff of this new organization, to be called Smith Farm Center for the Healing Arts. In true Michael style, he told me to not even think about my decision while I was on sabbatical, but to wait until I returned. I was already saying yes as he was talking; when I returned from Italy, I formally accepted his offer.

I have a master's degree in social work, with special training in family therapy, Gestalt therapy, and group theory and practice. My family therapy training gives me an understanding of how an illness affects all members of the system and what the possible repercussions may be. The Gestalt training has given me the ability to work directly with emotions, including fear, grief, and anger, as they arise. I have helped people access their emotions and move through them, so they come out in a different place.

So one year after I discovered an enlarged node in my left groin, I entered the world of healing. Since the fall of 1996 I have been on the staff of Smith Farm Center for the Healing Arts, and through my participation in that program, I have heard the stories of many people who have walked the cancer trail. I have performed several different functions within the organization, from intake/outtake worker to coleader. The coleader facilitates either the morning support group or the evening discussions, as well as offering individual time to each participant.

In the fall of 1997 I founded the New York Cancer Help Program. The program began by offering a support group to people with cancer, which included an hour of yoga, followed by an hour-and-a-half meeting of the support group. I was the facilitator of the group as well as director of the program, which was called Living Fully with Cancer. The program is committed to serving the multicultural, multiracial mix of New York City women. Some women participate for several years, some stay for a year or more, and some choose to stay through one cycle of seven meetings. Some people feel that once the cancer is gone they want to be away from that world. Other people have a fear of recurrence and want to stay in contact with a group of people who are in their position. Some people just like being there and keep coming for that reason; some people go back to work and cannot get time off. The only commitment we ask participants to make is to attend for seven weeks, at the start. My husband and I moved to Berkeley, California, in the winter of 2001 to be close to our children and grandchildren, but the group in New York has continued.

WHAT THIS BOOK OFFERS TO ITS READERS

In *The Etiquette of Illness* I explore the sensitivities that play a part in knowing how to respond when a person you care about becomes ill. I relate some experiences from the point of view of people who are sick and their responses to the care they receive. I have tried to convey what has worked and not worked for a number of real people in real situations. I show how the context of the relationship matters far more than the actual words that are used. I hope to expand awareness of the options, not give a blueprint. What I say to Joe may be different from what I say to John, depending on what I know of them and their individual circumstances and preferences.

By relating my experiences and the experiences of dozens of other people, I hope to suggest a range of helpful responses, so that next time you need to say, "I'm so sorry" or "How are you really doing?" You will find the words that are comfortable. I want to make it possible for those in the midst of pain and suffering to hear the warm intentions and concern in the voices of their friends, not judgments, prescriptions, fears, or neediness.

I use personal stories to expand awareness of how to respond to a friend with a serious illness by word (Chapter 1) and deed (Chapter 2). Stories illuminate how chronic illness gives rise to its own set of needs and responses. Chapter 3 presents stories of parents introducing children to death and dying, as well as parents talking to children about the parents' own illnesses. In Chapter 4 I focus on the issues that arise specifically around chronic illness. Chapter 5 is based on my conversations with doctors and patients about how their relationship works and what it takes to make it a healing exchange. And the final chapter tells stories of people who have reached out to their loved ones in the late stage of life and found the words with which to take leave. Throughout, I reflect on the underlying concepts that allow love and concern to show through in ways that are health giving for the sick person and affirming the giver.

I have made a decision in writing this book to use a few phrases instead of "patient." Patient connotes to me a sick body, lying in a bed, waiting for help that comes too late. That doesn't describe most of the people I know who are truly *living* with illness. I am uncomfortable with the term "survivor," as used for people with cancer, which makes me picture a person clawing his or her way up a beach after a shipwreck, half conscious, trying to make it to dry land. From all the people I have met in support groups, and all those I see in waiting rooms, what emerges is that we are simply people: people first, and dealing with a difficult, often life-

threatening condition second. Nearly all of us are valiant, coura-
geous, and full of life. Who I am as a person and who my fellow
journeyers are as people are far more dominant than what our
particular physical condition is on any given day. In the groups I
have had the privilege to facilitate, the humanness of the person is
far more important than the diagnosis. What kind of cancer, what
kind of treatment, is forgotten over the weeks of learning how
each person lives with his or her situation. And in the waiting
room it is often hard to tell who is carrying a disease and who is the
caregiver.

Instead of the word "patient," I have chosen perhaps clumsy
phrases, such as "person with cancer" or "the person with the
diagnosis." I do this to keep myself, and you, my reader, directly
aware of the individuality of those of whom I speak. Those terms
also prevent an "us and them" dichotomy, a sense that there are *the*
Well and *the* Sick. As I learned when unexpectedly, in midlife,
looking and feeling perfectly well, I was diagnosed with cancer,
illness can happen to anyone, anytime.

Only in the chapter "Patients Talk to Doctors; Doctors Talk to
Patients" do I refer to people who are sick as patients, because it is
linguistically in balance in with doctors and accurately describes
the relationship.

ẻ

Usually etiquette means simply a correct form of speech and
behavior to be used in predictable situations. I use the word in

a different sense in this book. I intend etiquette to mean thoughtful and compassionate behaviors, influenced by the specifics of
care and relationship. This book will show you ways to interact
with sincerity and kindness with friends and loved ones who are ill.
It offers many options from which you may choose what suits you.
There is no *one* correct way to write the perfect card or say the
perfect words of condolence. What is important is to be able to
write the card, when you are so moved. And once you have
written, to send the card, to make the call, to ask your questions,
to give voice to your feelings of love.

The "well person" often feels helpless when a friend or relative
receives a difficult medical diagnosis. Our friend is sick and we
want to fix it. We are filled with the desire to do *something*—and to
do it "right." Many times words desert us. People have often asked
me, "What should I say?" It is to this question that my book
responds in myriad ways, large and small.

I wrote this book to offer my insights on how to respond to
friends, neighbors, loved ones, and even strangers in times of
suffering. And I wrote it for those of us who are seriously ill,
engaged in our own journey of healing. I hope that these stories
will make it easier for us both, when we are receiving and when we
are giving care, to find the way to hear the good intentions and
concern of those around us.

Throughout this book, I illustrate a given situation by offering
things to say that worked in this context. These phrases are not
meant to be memorized and played back verbatim. Rather, they

are offered as a catalyst to help you open yourself to a variety of phrases to use with your particular friend or loved one. What I offer are not the only possible answers to, "What should I say?" but are a small ray of light that I hope will penetrate readers and illuminate their own heartfelt words for these confounding moments.

1. Finding the Words

Yes, the natural way is always best.
If you are going to make noise
It is better to rumble like the rocks
Than to tinkle like artificial jade.
                                    —Lao Tzu

I stand with my hand on the receiver. I want to call my friend who has just been diagnosed with lupus, but my mind has reverted to that of a seven-year-old, and an inner tape plays, "What am I going to say? How am I going to say it? Who will I find on the end of the phone? The friend I have always known? Or my friend who is sick, in a state I have never heard before, and I won't know what to say?" I have learned from experience that I need to do something when someone is on my mind, but once again I find myself in this anxiety zone. As I do each time, I forget that I am calling my friend, the calm, unflappable, funny Ginny, who has lupus, and instead I feel that I am calling someone named Lupus, whom I do not know. To my relief, as soon as my friend's voice comes on the line, my memory of our connection kicks in, of course, and we talk as we always have.

The thing to remember is that when you finally do talk to your friend, she will be bringing her whole self, the self you already know so well. All you have to do is listen. You have a relationship. You have a past that includes shared experiences, friends in common, subjects you have talked about. You know your friend's likes and dislikes, you know what pleases her and annoys her. Just call. Once she answers, there will be two of you on the call; it will not all be up to you.

≈

Recently, I had lunch with my friend Carol Anne in Mill Valley, California. We were in a café bookshop, looking out on a brick wall, where there was a true-to-life mural of the golden hills of California, dotted with the deep greens of the live oak trees. As a tattooed young waitress brought us our Tuscan bread soup, Carol Anne told me that she had been angry at her friend Sarah. Though Sarah clearly knew that Carol Anne had received a cancer diagnosis and was undergoing treatment, she had not phoned for months. Finally, one day, Carol Anne answered the phone and heard Sarah's voice. Sarah said to her, "I am so sorry it took me so long to call, but I didn't know what to say to you."

"That is all you had to say," Carol Anne said. "That's all you have to say." At that, the eyes of both women welled up with tears. Carol Anne thanked Sarah for calling and told her how much it meant to her to hear from her, and how she had missed her, and been angry with her, and felt abandoned. But, Carol Anne told

Sarah, what she had just said, "I don't know what to say," was all she had to say. Just to be in contact with Sarah, just to hear in Sarah's voice her wish to make everything all right, resolved Carol Anne's anger and reconnected their friendship.

Let this be your guide. Just the simple phrase, "I don't know what to say" can be the catalyst, and everything will flow from there.

Of course we don't know what to say. Life does not prepare us for the blow that bad news brings. We don't want to make it worse, we don't want to frighten our loved ones with our anxiety, we don't want to voice our worst fears, and yet we need to call. There is no training program for what to say, and some of us, happily, have very little experience. Some people I have met have felt abandoned in hard times by good friends. Sometimes people who are ill and feeling abandoned will call the friends they miss, but that is rare. It is the role of the "well person" to reach out. While it can be hard to initiate contact, doing so brings pleasure and solace to both parties.

❧

Another rather different story tells the same tale. A young man of nineteen heard that his aunt, whom he loved, had cancer and was not doing well. He was an awkward, unsure teenager who did not say much to adults. One day his aunt's phone rang, and she picked up the receiver to hear the voice of her nephew Jonathon saying, "I don't know what to say to you, but I just had to call you. I hope that's all right." The woman held tight to the phone, not wanting to lose this precious moment with this dear young man, who was doing so well what so many of us are afraid of doing. Just reaching out.

ン☙

Before calling a friend with a serious illness, especially if I know very little about the disease, I find I can listen with more understanding if I do my research first. There are a number of good medical sources on the Internet; you can easily type in the name of the disease and learn a great deal. Every bookstore and library has books with information on symptoms, treatments, and prognosis. Then, when I call my friend, I am better equipped to understand what is happening to her. It's not my task to correct her. I just understand the details better if I have a framework.

ン☙

How often should you call? If you are thinking about your sick friend all day long, call and tell him or just check in. If you feel you have put it off too long, then call now. If you feel you have called too often, then ask what he thinks. Instead of asking him to call you back, just call and say, "Thinking of you." It means so much to come home to those messages. When I had been out at doctor appointments for the day, to be greeted at my apartment by the messages of friends made me feel held in a cocoon of care. Waiting rooms are depersonalized. We are all just bodies, waiting for a machine to see the imperfections of that body. To return home to the reality of love in my life took away the cold, windowless waiting of the day.

When should you call? Call anytime. Most people have answering machines, and people who are unwell learn when they can and cannot take calls. Ringers can be turned off. The volume can be turned down. What I know from my own experience is that I was comforted in times of difficulty by a phone message. I liked to hear the sound of friends' voices, their characteristic ways of speaking. It was so nice to come home and receive messages at my own pace, to know that my friends had thought of me that day. I especially liked getting short messages that required no answer. If I was too tired even to listen to the calls, Charlie, my husband, would listen, respond to those that required a response, and, when I was ready, tell me about them.

❧

Answering phone messages is a great job for the caregiver who is willing and available. Caregivers need to feel that they are making a difference, and for me, at least, it was a major relief to have my husband respond to calls. While undergoing radiation I continued to work at a job that kept me on the telephone for long periods of time during the day. To come home at night to answer more calls and return messages was draining. Charlie, though he talked on the phone all day too, found the calls at home engaging, and he enthusiastically relieved me of the personal calls. Then together we could delight in the circle of support that formed around us. An unexpected benefit of Charlie's role was that he too was bolstered by the calls. Many people thought to ask after him, and as he went with me to many doctor appointments and shaped his work and travel life around my appointments and needs, he too needed comfort, recognition, and love. Phone calls were a great way for both of us to receive care.

Charlie also took on the task of updating the message on the answering machine, asking callers to leave messages, sometimes giving the current health report, and telling people that they might not get a call back, depending on my energy. This meant that people who called received answers to their questions and could let us know they cared, but they did not expect a call back. Particularly during the early period of finding doctors, getting second opinions, and making decisions, this practice helped both of us.

❧

There are other ways to send your thoughts. Cards are always welcome. A card can be cherished, saved, and reread, and it needs no response. People display their cards on a table, hang them over the fireplace, or share them with others. They can be saved to be read again and again, and children can read them in later years. I heard about a young man whose wife died suddenly, and many people wrote to him. At the time he couldn't bear to open the cards, but he saved them. He knew who had written, and that was enough for him. He kept the cards together in a box, waiting for the time when he was ready.

There are get-well cards at stores that may help, if the words do not come to you, though there are no cards for people who aren't going to get well. Writing your own card requires entering fully into your feelings about your friend. The following are suggestions to help you move into what you want to say.

I am so sorry this is happening to you.
I can't stop thinking about you.
I will pray for you.
I keep remembering that time we . . .
I look forward to being with you again.

Each time the card is read, the writer is present with the reader, over and over again.

❧

Months ago, when Martin was at a program far away from home, his dear friend Paula's husband died. Martin had known that her husband could die while he was away, and he had kept in close touch with Paula. And when Sandor did die, Martin wrote an e-mail, that being the fastest, easiest way to relay his feelings. He tried hard to convey his grief over Sandor's death and his sadness at not being with Paula. He said that he was sorry to be so far away at this time. He wished to be near Paula, to hold her, to hug her, to mourn with her.

Martin had not had to write many such letters, and he was

worried about getting it just right. Was he putting his needs before Paula's? Why would Paula want to hear about Martin's sadness? Did not she have enough of her own? Was this truly a way for Martin to be helpful? To me, it sounded like a wonderful e-mail, and just what Paula would want to hear—how her friend Martin was feeling at this moment about her loss and Sandor's death. Because we are so unsure of what works, and because we get too little feedback, we sometimes forget that the expression of true loving feelings is always right.

Find the qualities in your friend that you love. Putting into words what we like about another person is not always easy. Yet it is such a gift to receive validation of who we are to somebody else. This is often the value of cards and e-mails: In writing we are free to be more expressive than in person. Whether your medium is the written or spoken word, trying to articulate what you like about your friend, or what you admire about him in this situation may be useful. It may be courage, resilience, tenacity, humor, warmth, generosity, kindness, gentleness, strength, vivacity, joy of living, willingness to take risks, being a good parent, or being lovable— everyone has positive qualities. It only takes mention of a characteristic to remind your friend of all that you appreciate in him.

ॐ

What words we say depend on the individual, the relationship, and our level of consciousness. But it is bound to be satisfying to both parties if we express our compassion truthfully, from our hearts.

The ability to express the truth in one's heart develops over time. As I write that phrase, I am reminded of a conversation I had with my mother when I was sixteen, about to go out on a date with a boy I liked. I asked her what I should talk about with him, and she replied, "Just be yourself, dear." I had no idea what that meant. The *me* from summertime, the *me* from class, the *me* with my best friend Joanie, the *me* who read under my blankets after the lights were turned out? It took years of trial and error to feel I was being true to myself, years of acting like someone else, of trying on being serious one day, funny another, times of being too helpful, occasions of being too distant—until I was able to review all the attempts and discover how to be simply who I am in the moment.

There are actual physical methods to help us find our own voices. One colleague of mine teaches her clients to touch their sternum with their right hand as a way of engaging their own truths. Some people find themselves by putting their hands near their hearts, facilitating the path inward. I turn my internal eye to my solar plexis, deep down into my own center of feeling, to determine what is happening for me that needs to be expressed. If standing, you can try leaning forward onto the balls of your feet. If seated, lean forward in your chair. In these different postures, see whether words come more easily than in more passive positions. Play with the possibilities to find your own way.

❧

Many of us fear that we will say the wrong thing. This fear is what stands in the way of picking up the telephone. I have one friend who will never forget saying to a man with one hand, "I have to hand it to you . . ." Not long ago, I put my foot in my mouth. Here is the story.

My friend Jackie, who lives in Toronto, planned a visit to San Francisco. We were to see each other for the third time in the forty-five years since we used to spend summers at camp together. When Jackie arrived in the airport in San Francisco, she noticed large raised red welts appearing on her hands and arms. She immediately went to a Red Cross station in the airport and showed the welts to a doctor on duty, who rushed her off to the hospital. She was told she could not leave the hospital, as she might have a life-threatening condition, and she spent the night in a hospital bed.

I received a message from Jackie that morning on my answering machine in Berkeley: "Don't come to the hotel to meet me; I'm at UCSF Medical Center." I tried calling her, but she was out of her room having tests. So I left immediately to go meet her at the hospital.

While Jackie waited for the results of her electrocardiogram, I sat with her and we talked that morning about our experiences together at summer camp in Canada, forty-five years earlier. But I also told her, in the course of the morning, about my friend Nancy's mother, who, en route to visit her daughter at college, died of a heart attack in the airport. I told my friend Jackie this story while she was lying waiting for the results of an electro-cardiogram, after having symptoms suggestive of heart problems at the airport. This was not a good story for that day, or that person. It's understandable that I thought of it, but what made it come out of me?

We all have stories of saying the wrong thing that still make us shudder months or years later. But really the answer is to be both more conscious and more comfortable. When we are nervous about what to say, the mind can produce material that might seem to make the situation worse. Yet when I checked with Jackie, she didn't remember me telling her any story that was inappropriate. I was reminded not to be so afraid of what I say, yet at the same time to try to be more judicious in my choice of comments.

As for her health, Jackie was cleared of all possible heart problems in the course of the morning and went off to enjoy her time in San Francisco. When I saw her six months later, she was in perfect health.

ॐ

Some people who have many recurrences of illness and many hospitalizations, and who also have many friends, work out phone trees and assistance networks. Kathy, who lived in Pittsburgh, had a team of close friends who wrote letters to everyone who had reached out to Kathy in any way. The group of friends had a team name and an emblem printed on T-shirts. There is no doubt in my mind that Kathy lived longer because of their support, and that her end was softened by this team of friends, some of whom had not known each other before her illness.

A small group of friends can create a network in which each is responsible for informing a few other people about the changes, appointments, results of tests, level of anxiety, and even the needs of the person who is ill. When actual service is needed—food, assistance, or care—the network is in place to help.

When I first found the lump in my groin, I went to some doctors' appointments alone. I sat in waiting rooms alone, and I managed. But I soon learned that waiting is so much better when someone was with me. The time goes faster. It feels less like a personal affront when the PET scan machine breaks and a friend and I wait an extra hour together. It becomes more like a date than a wait. I'm hugely grateful to friends who came with me, met me, stayed with me, checked on me, during long afternoons of scans, infusions, and sitting. It was a joy to be with them. Often, they said words that touched my heart.

&

For many people who are ill, it's affirming to be reminded that they are still attractive people. For example, I think of Kaitlin. She was newly separated from her husband, and a very young-looking fifty. Kaitlin had colon cancer. This is a serious diagnosis, and she had an unusual cancer, with a poor prognosis. She traveled to Mexico and Switzerland seeking alternative treatments, as well as doing several rounds of experimental chemotherapy in New York City, where she lived.

Kaitlin sparkled. Bald at times, or with curly red locks at others, she came into a room and light spun off her. It was as though she showered in glitter and then, borne on air, went from one healing event to the next, spreading her light. About two months before she died, Kaitlin went to Paris on her way back from a treatment in Zurich. In a hotel dining room, she met an attractive Frenchman who bought her a drink and then, upon her invitation, came to her table. They talked all through dinner. Afterward, he bought her a rose and walked her upstairs to her room. She was thin by then, and crisscrossed with abdominal surgery. At the door to her room the man kissed her, and she let him know that was all there would be. But the pleasure it gave her to appear desirable was as life giving as any medical treatment.

Kaitlin's story shows the value of compliments, flirting, admiring, appreciating your sick friend out loud, just as you used to do before she was sick. Kaitlin received this attention from a stranger, but friends can do it as well. Don't let the loving, lusting, adorable side of your friend disappear. It was very satisfying to have my friends continue to treat me as an attractive woman even when I looked less than well. And I was delighted when my doctor, on seeing me bald for the first time, said, "On you, that really works. You look great."

❧

It is possible to make respectful suggestions. I have been recommending that you listen and support in all instances, but there are occasions where some positive input can truly be helpful. One valuable thing friends can contribute, in walking the path with us, is to remind us of the larger picture and to offer motivation to help us through the hard times.

When I received my cancer diagnosis, my friend Lauren dared to say to me that she hoped I would work less hard now that I had cancer in my life. My friend Deborah told me she hoped I would take time to travel with my husband more, now that I was working less. They both offered these reflections with care and love, not as imperatives, but as possibilities.

I knew a woman, a blonde, lighthearted beauty, who had facial surgery for basal cell carcinoma. When I saw her on the second day of her recovery, she had black stitches around her nose. She was deeply concerned, since she was a performer and needed to be able to be looked at with ease. That day, she was angry at the doctor and worried about her career, the reactions of others, and how she was going to face the world. In the grip of the procedures and their immediate results, she seemed to have forgotten that if left unattended, the cancer would have eaten away a portion of her face and might even have threatened her life. When I reminded her why she had had the surgery, her sensible self rose up. Soon after, she went out into the world, her head up, ready to face down the stares and radiate her inner glory. Over the next weeks the stitches were removed, the scarring diminished, some more plastic work was done, and she is her gorgeous self again.

❧

For about seven months of my life, in 2000 and again in 2003, I was either bald or had extremely short hair. Some good friends told me I looked great, which made me feel wonderful. Some people didn't know what to say. Some acted like I looked as I normally did. Some people looked at me a millisecond longer than they used to and then looked away. It was a lesson in what people with visible disabilities face every day of their lives.

There is an implicit cultural norm in North America that dictates that we not take any notice of people who look different. For me, bald, I felt more exposed, vulnerable, noticeable than ever before in my life. I wanted to acknowledge the change, but I didn't want to say much. Concerned with my health, I became much less concerned about my looks than ever before; at the same time, I was told I looked better than ever. It was very confusing.

People appeared to treat my no-hair style as though it were a choice, a fashion statement. I used to think that I looked healthy enough for it to be a fashion choice, but now, as I look at pictures of myself bald, I see a person dealing with a serious illness—AIDS or cancer. Yet few people feel able to ask about the underlying illness; it's easier to talk about superficial changes. We all want everything to be all right and so we may choose not to comment on the obvious. In many cases, however, a respectful question or comment about the sickness will be welcome, a relief to both parties.

The sick person may handle physical changes in a variety of ways, and all of them are fine. In my case, I was uncomfortable in turbans and in the wig I bought. I never felt that the wig was sitting straight. I wanted to tug it one way or another. It gave me a claustrophobic headache. Being bald allowed me to wear a small hat that I could put on and take off, depending on temperature and drafts. I needed to do what felt most comfortable to me. Other people in similar situations would not consider going out in public without a wig or hat. Many people go to jobs where it would be uncomfortable for them to be bald. I wasn't in a situation like this, however. What I realized was that everyone who saw me was having a different reaction. There was no way that I could please them all. So I decided to please myself.

While I was bald, I went to a Christmas party in my apartment building in New York, where my husband and I had lived for twelve years. When I arrived, four women surrounded me and talked vigorously about our upcoming move to California and the sale of our apartment but never about the fact that I was suddenly, noticeably shiny and bald on top. Then our neighbor Alan came in, who knew me no more or less well than the others, and said, "Oh Susan, I didn't know you were having a hard winter. How are you doing?" If I hadn't wanted to talk about it, I could have changed the subject. But I found this a great opening, a great relief. Everyone moved in and listened to my answer. And then small talk, general conversations, other topics flowed. It was, for me, a refreshing acknowledgment of reality. I could easily imagine myself doing what the women had done, but now I know the value of doing as Alan did.

Here are some of the ways you could address the subject of a friend's illness:

What is this like for you?
I see that the condition has left some changes.
I am sorry you are facing this life change.
Do you want to talk about your condition?

Any of these questions or comments recognize the situation and would give your friend comfort.

❧

Sometimes this kind of gentle concern is welcome, even from strangers. A woman at a Jewish Friday evening service turned to me and said, "I hope you don't mind my asking, but have you just completed some kind of treatment?"

I didn't mind at all; I was delighted to have her ask, and we talked and talked. She had just visited her former college roommate, who had finished chemotherapy about the same time I did. Her friend's hair was about a third of an inch long, like mine, she said, and I reminded her of her friend. Very comfortably, she went on to ask me about my course of treatment, my reactions to it, my choice of going bareheaded, and how I felt at that point. I was touched by her interest. The experience was so fresh to me, and it was still so central to my thoughts, that a chance to talk about it was precious to me. I had just moved to California and missed my daily connections to my friends in New York, so this woman's attention was very welcome. I must, in some way, have let her know that this conversation would please me. I don't usually engage with strangers in this way and would not welcome it a year later. Yet that night, it worked so well.

Similarly, at one conference I went to, a stunning young woman came up and threw her arms around me. I reminded her so much of her mother, she said, who had chosen to remain bald during treatment, that she just needed to hug me. I loved it. She loved it. I would never have initiated such a thing—it's just not my way—but it was so true to this young woman that it worked.

❧

It's not just words that count; tone of voice matters too. It's dismaying for most people who are dealing with illness when they are greeted with cries of, "Oh, oh my God, this is so terrible!" Or when people ask, in stricken tones, "How *are* you?" The minor key does not sit well with people who are trying to be hopeful. As a sick person, I don't want to be responsible for cheering you up. I don't want you to treat me as a problem. I want a more neutral, curious approach that allows me to reveal what I want. I may need to be strong with you one day and to explore my fears with you the next. One woman in my group changed her mind about attending a well-known national program for people with cancer because the intake worker started by asking her, fearfully, "How *are* you?" To this woman, the intake worker's voice implied that the world was ending and the woman was not going make it.

Family and friends, out of their own desire to fix, cure, and be helpful, often give advice:

Drink this tea; take this medicine or supplement.
Call this person; he or she is the healer for you.
You have to get that bone marrow transplant, it's the only
    way.
I won't help you if you refuse to . . .

These directives arise from the best of intentions, but they are not respectful of the needs of the diagnosed person. The person with the disease is trying to make sense of all the options put forth by his or her doctor and in the literature, not to mention other people who have been through the same thing. There are choices to be made about conventional treatment, alternative treatment, and complementary care. The person who is facing an illness needs to find his own way and make his own choices. It is very different to say, "Here is some information I have that makes sense to me; see what you think," than to say, "You've got to do this," "Take my word for it, this is what you should do," or "I don't know why you're not doing as I say."

For parents with sick adult children, allowing their offspring the space to make choices is especially hard. For people in the medical profession with sick relatives, it is nearly impossible. But to people who are actively making treatment decisions, telephone messages with instant remedies and insistent claims are an additional burden, not a support. People who are making treatment decisions do not want to hurt the feelings of those who are hoping to be helpful, but I will tell you from the inside, that unasked-for advice sets up strong resistance. Even if you have a useful idea, it's hard to hear if it is put forth as must-do advice rather than a choice. It's more constructive to offer yourself as a sounding board and then let your friend or relative come to you.

෭

As I suggested in my story about my friend Jackie, who was rushed to the hospital in San Francisco, an area that needs to be handled with care is that moment when someone's story triggers in your memory a similar, but worse, story. Gary tore his ligament in a race and went to the medical tent for ice. The doctor in charge spent five minutes telling him about the terrible accident the doctor's own wife had with her ligament the previous week, which was the last thing Gary wanted to hear right then. When people are suffering, they're not open to hearing horror stories about others with similar maladies. There is less capacity for compassion at such moments. Gary just wanted some ice.

On the other hand, stories of miraculous recoveries can be extremely welcome. When my aunt Edith, at age eighty-nine, had her legs broken in a golf-cart accident, what meant the most to her was a visit from a nurse in the hospital who had had an identical accident a few years before. Aunt Edith was lying still in her bed motionless, afraid to move in case she might injure herself more. One of the broken legs could not be put in a cast, since there was an open wound on it. She was fearful of what lay ahead for her. She liked to golf, dance in her high heels, and go to Arizona every winter, and she had no idea whether she'd be able to do these things again. But then this nurse came to visit, walking into the room without a limp, and told her story, which was similar to Aunt Edith's and ended with complete recovery. Aunt Edith spoke of the nurse's visit for days after the event. The hope the nurse offered Aunt Edith buoyed her spirits and, I am sure, sped her healing.

ॐ

Confidentiality may be an important issue for people who get sick. People may not want it known what their condition is. People may desire privacy for personal reasons, or to protect their professional lives. We need to respect their wishes.

Confidentiality is especially important in the work world. Cancer is becoming less stigmatized than it was ten years ago, but it still may be a matter for secrecy, shame, silence, and even fear. When the cancer is life-threatening, many people do not want it known at the office unless they are ready to stop working. I've heard stories of people feeling passed over for promotions because it was thought that their health was too fragile, even though the diagnosed person expected to be able to handle the new job. People who rely on word of mouth to bring them clients fear that they will lose clients or customers if their illness becomes public. Psychotherapists, for example, think long and hard about when to tell their patients—and their colleagues—they are ill. It is entirely within the right of the person who is ill to determine who knows and who does not.

It is tempting, with illness, to quickly pass on what we know. But it's important to check carefully each time to learn whether the person with the diagnosis wants it known. Why do we violate the privacy of others so freely with illness? Is it a need to share our deeper fear and distress? Is it to verify that we are safe, and it is someone else's misfortune? Is it a kind of prayer for them? It is all of these things. But it is also not our place to relieve our discomfort by intruding on someone else's privacy.

❧

There is too little attention given to feedback in the caregiving, caretaking domain. How much goodwill is spread around when we thank a friend for a comment, card, or call that touched us. To let people know that what they said worked for you gives them encouragement to say something meaningful to someone else. How can we find comfort with our responses to suffering if we do not let each other know what works?

As I was working on this manuscript at a retreat at the Rockefeller Foundation's Villa Serbelloni, in Bellagio, Italy, I heard touching stories. Because there was a lot of talk about what we were each working on, far more than in my everyday life, and because I spent so much time with the other twenty-four residents of the program, over a month's time there were opportunities for many exchanges and much follow-up. People knew what I was writing, and this elicited several of the stories I have included here. I also told people that I had had cancer and was recovering from chemotherapy, that my supershort hair was not a choice but rather the result of six weeks' growth. Because I am an expert in this area of what to say, both from my work in many settings with people with cancer and from my own interest in this subject, some of the Bellagio fellows found addressing me about my illness daunting.

In the first week I was there, a group of eight of us took a ferryboat across Lake Como, from Bellagio to Varenne, late one afternoon, to see the gardens at the Monastero. Ron walked with me and gently, quietly he asked how I was doing. I was so touched. He was hesitant yet interested. He told me about a good friend of his who had received cancer treatment at the same time as I had and how she was doing. I felt so cared for by his asking this simple question and offering up his distress about his friend. We were walking through the village square surrounded by plane trees that had been pollarded to provide deep shade from the summer sun. The church steeple was one of the beauties of the region. The town was old, the roofs were all of red tile, and the townspeople were out soaking up the early spring sunshine. Ron and I walked together slowly, separate from the rest of the group, and I thought, "It won't be so difficult being with all these strangers for a month, bald and recovering."

The next day I thanked Ron for his question about my state of health, and he was so relieved. This is why I make a case for feedback. Ron is a writer. He knows words. He writes beautifully and has had several books published, and yet even he was not sure he had it "right." I assured him he had been wonderful, that it is less the words than the simple attention: "How are you?" Ron tried, and was unsure, and I had not realized that I put him on the spot with my expert stance. Feedback on both sides helps. Let the following ideas help you find your own words:

This works . . .
That doesn't work.
That was hard to say.
Did I do okay?

"Thank you" goes a long way. It is hard to learn new behaviors when sick, but expressing appreciation is a necessity, especially if long-term help is needed. Caregivers can get worn down if they are taken for granted. In the busy lives we all lead, anyone who steps outside of his or her own set of demands for even a moment to aid another deserves immediate and perhaps repeated thanks.

I heard about a woman who made dinners each week for a sick friend and her husband and left them at their door, without even going in to visit. She was glad to be able to do this for her friends, and she was kept going by the appreciation she received. Her sick friend even had flowers sent as thanks for the homemade dinners.

When I care for people in the hospital and they say, "Thanks," it makes all the difference in my ability to keep on staying with them.

Just the word "thanks" goes a long way. Describing how it feels to receive, as specifically as possible, is useful as well. Many of us did not grow up knowing how to receive graciously, or to give to others in their time of need. If people who are sick talk more about their difficulty receiving, and how much it means to have friends give in ways that are pleasurable, it helps the giver plan his or her own giving. You could say

> I am so touched. I feel strange being so helpless, and you
>   helped me without taking away my independence.
> This means so much to me.
> Having you with me made it better.

Comments such as these encourage the giver to give more. There is no need to go on and on. A simple "thank you" will do. But at least one "thank you" is very important. Sometimes people feel overwhelmed by gratitude. They feel they can never do for the other what has been done for them. They become paralyzed and pull out of the friendship. I hope you will find the way to receive fully, believing that the giver would not do more than he or she wishes to do.

❧

I remember stumbling up the hill outside the hospital after my fifteenth of twenty radiation treatments. I fell into a cab, found my way to the train in Grand Central Station through shrouds of black fatigue, and ended up north of New Haven, Connecticut. My friends live on top of a hill looking down past West Rock, out to Long Island Sound and even to Long Island on a clear day. The next morning, my friend Kate drew a hot bath for me and left me to soak. Afterward, I lay on her giant white bed, looking out over the autumn leaves all the way to the water, reading, curled up with her big black Labrador retriever, Sophie. Kate wrapped me up in blankets and left me to recover. There is no way I can give this back to Kate. I had to let it in that she wanted to do this for me, revel in the comfort, and let her know how wonderful this experience was for me.

Of course, we all know people who ask and receive all too well. With them we need to draw limits on what we give. Julie was depressed by the weight of fear she experienced when she received her diagnosis. She lay in bed and was angry at anyone who was happy or laughing or appeared to be well. She did not give to those around her as she used to, and she expected to be loved and cared for. She expected to be the center of her household of four women without making her usual contributions, though she had no symptoms or physical disability. Her roommates tolerated this behavior for three weeks before they began to expect her to take up her some of her household duties again. They began to set limits on the amount of time she could expect them to listen to her complain about the world going on without her. She was angry at them at first, but she later reported that without their setting limits on her behavior, she might never have risen up out of her bed again.

More frequent, in my life, are people who do not expect to be cared for and have trouble taking it in when it comes. I had this problem myself at the beginning of my time with cancer. One of the big lessons of the illness for me has been that it is a gift to allow someone else to do something for me when I need it. The mutual pleasure that occurs with receiving can be a transformative experience for each. There are chances for me now to rebalance the equation by giving to those who ask for my attention.

❧

I was surprised to learn that Patricia, who is a successful doctor, had trouble telling a solicitous colleague that he was calling too often when she was sick and that his questions felt like a cross-examination. What might she have said to slow him down? Perhaps, "I am doing pretty well these days. I need to take care of myself in my own way." Or, "Thanks so much for your calls, but the best thing you could do for me is to call a little less. I appreciate your attention, and now I just need quiet." This too is feedback, and it's what was needed in that relationship. To protect herself, Patricia might have told the giver what would truly help. Without this feedback, he didn't know and didn't have the opportunity to fine-tune his behavior.

There are people who give others their bone marrow, a kidney, or their blood. There is no wrong way to thank the people who make these sacrifices. The only possible mistake is not thanking them enough. Expressing feelings of gratitude does not make us weak; it may make us stronger. Sometimes a look, a smile, a touch is enough to convey deep thanks. Two people participate in the exchange of care, and both have a part to play. There is a lot of power in acknowledging the gift. The engagement, the connection, the two sides of the exchange make the receiving easier for the receiver and the giver.

ﻬ

Allison told her friend Jan about her cancer. But Allison was not ready to tell her own sister, because she expected her sister to be very frightened, and this feeling would probably give rise to a rush of advice and information. Allison did not feel strong enough to manage her sister's panic. She was just starting to gather her own information and needed to do it her way, in her time. Her priorities were different from her sister's; she was much more interested in alternative care.

Against Allison's wishes, Jan told Allison's sister, who immediately called Allison. Allison was in bed that day. Her sister wanted to have a discussion. "Is it okay that Jan told me?" she asked. Allison had the presence of mind to say no, but her sister continued anyway. Having made one true self-protective statement and not being heard, Allison gave up and tried to listen to the stream of advice. This went on for too long, and then the conversation was over. Allison felt steamrolled by her sister and betrayed by her friend. The next time she spoke to Jan she told her that she had not been ready to hear from her sister just yet and hoped that Jan understood.

This story is an example of a relationship that was difficult to begin with and was exacerbated by Allison's illness. Allison could have been stronger with her sister. She could have tried saying, "This is too much for me now. You know we differ about treatment methods, and I need to do it my way this time, and I need you to support me in my choices. I have trouble when we disagree this way; can we please not get into this discussion about my treatment? You would be most helpful to me if you'd just agree with me about everything for a few weeks." Any of these statements might have offered Allison the protection she needed, without being confrontational. At this vulnerable moment, she could not say them. Later, as she felt physically stronger, Allison stopped letting her sister walk all over her.

Sometimes we have a friend or relative we have always had a difficult relationship with. It is within your rights to see less of that person during times of illness or crisis. We know who has a healing presence and who does not, and a politely stated, "No, not now," can be a necessary self-protection. It is reasonable to say, "I'm not ready to see you right now," "I don't want to make any plans at the moment," "I am managing well on my own," "I find I need a lot of time alone, and am not making social plans," or "I look forward to seeing you in a few months." Make choices about what suits you and then, in a careful, polite way, make it happen. There are ways to manage our time with people who do not fit comfortably with our state of being. We can see them with a group of people, or less often.

ॐ

In close, loving relationships we sometimes expect others to know how to comfort us when we are hurting. But they often feel they don't know how, or won't get it right, or may even exacerbate the problem. Some people feel frightened by tears, or expressions of unhappiness, pain, and fear. They pull away. Thinking they may make things worse, they disappear. The person who wants support needs to teach the words and postures of comfort. What do you like to hear when you are aching?

I am here with you through this.
You are perfect just the way you are.
It is okay to cry.
Take your time with your sadness.
You don't have to be cheerful all the time with me.
I love you.

Find the words that give you comfort and teach your friends to say them. Tell your loved one whether you want to be held in a lap or in arms, or touched, stroked, patted, or caressed. Or do you not want to be touched? The important thing is to get an image of what you need or want and communicate that desire to your loved one.

Tears arise in many different circumstances and elicit many different reactions. They may give rise to compassion or love in the heart of those witnessing the tears. They may bring tears to the eyes of the watchers. They may bring a great sense of relief to both parties. Tears can also seem needy, insatiable, unstoppable, terrifying. They may arise in moments of joy as well as times of sorrow. For some people tears are rare and hard to come by.

How to respond to a person who is crying has as many possibilities as there are people. Some people disappear into their busy lives, their fear. Some people stay and try to talk away the tears. And people who are crying need different things as well. The offer of a handkerchief can be helpful for certain people, but to others might mean, "I need you to stop crying now." The words, "You'll be okay" and "There, there," are common offerings. Each of us wants different words when crying. These words can be taught. We can think about what words are comforting to us and teach them to those who are likely to be with us in tearful moments:

I'm here with you.
Yes, yes.
Let them come.
I am so sad for you.
Yes, this is very hard.

Saying one phrase over and over can feel like a caress. The tears come in waves. Staying quietly present can be reassuring.

Silent holding is often the best. You don't need to have words to make it all right. The tears may be the best thing there is. It is not a time for correction, interpretation, or attitude adjustments. It is a time for love and respect for whatever the crier is feeling. Tears wash the heart. Tears can be a way to release emotion and move forward. They can relieve pressure. Tears can be an outlet for thoughts and feelings that have no words. They should not be cut off, choked back, or denied. There is no need to run away. They will stop. This is a guarantee.

❧

I met Helen while traveling in France. Her beautiful, straight, shiny red hair was falling out. Clumps of it fell out each day when she washed, combed, or touched it. Tufts were coming back in white, in the midst of the auburn. The doctors had told her it was unclear whether her hair would ever return to normal. The comments she found hardest to hear were the ones that stated categorically, "This will stop," "You'll be fine," "Don't worry," "It will grow back, I know it will," "I know this will be over soon," and "You will get better, I know it."

These comments do not help. They are an expression of the needs of the giver, not the receiver. They are undermining, not supportive, denying a difficult reality. They demand correction by the receiver, which is hard to do in the moment, and then the moment passes. Thoughtfulness is needed on both sides. It is okay for anyone whose toes are stepped on to speak about his or her feelings immediately or when next they meet. "I didn't like it when I saw you last time and you said, 'You'll be fine, I know you will.' That doesn't work very well for me." That is all that is needed. It is hard to do this, but without feedback, we can never learn.

☙

It was a year after Anna's treatment for an early-stage breast cancer had ended. She was examining her life in depth and trying to figure out what she would like to do with her work life and her love life. There had been a lot of breast cancer in her family, a lot of recurrence, and a lot of death. She was trying to keep an open mind about that and not assume it was her destiny as well. Yet she wanted to do everything she could to prevent a recurrence. She was in a support group and used the services of a number of complementary healers to assist in her recovery and maintenance of good health. One day her sister-in-law asked her, "When are you going to get over this and get on with your life?" Anna was deeply hurt. She was taking good care of herself, trying to make difficult choices about her work and her life, and she was very fearful about a recurrence. Having her sister-in-law rush her through her process was disturbing to her.

I offer here several replies to the kind of comment Anna's sister-in-law made, so you can find the words that suit your personality and the relationship in the moment when they are needed.

> I hear how distressed you are with my slow recovery.
> I hear how worried you are about me.
> I am sorry that I cannot respond to that.
> I need another twenty years to recover.
> There is no time limit on recovery.
> I'll let you know when I know.
> That is not a question you can ask.
> I find that very hurtful.
> I can't answer that question.
> What is it you are trying to say to me?

਼ੈ

I met Tessa in a group for women with cancer. She had just finished her treatments for breast cancer, which included a double mastectomy. Tessa is forty years old, a hospice worker, and the mother of a nine-year-old boy. She has a lovely warm, welcoming face and now once again has her thick, dark, short hair.

Matter-of-fact, always calm, and well-grounded, Tessa is often more concerned about other people than herself. She acts like she can handle anything. She would like to live a slower-paced life than before, but she also feels called to continue her work as a physical and spiritual guide.

Tessa liked her beautiful full breasts. She took pictures of them before and after the operation. After deep and careful soul-searching, she chose not to have reconstructive surgery. She hoped that with exercise, she could enlarge her pectoral muscles enough to create a nice look of some softness, in and out of clothing. In keeping with her new look, Tessa bought a black maillot bathing suit, with narrow straps and a smooth flat body. In her simple, elegant suit, Tessa felt and looked like a firm young adolescent. She liked the look and feel of her new body. It had an appeal all its own. Her husband liked her new look too. Nothing hurt, everything was working. She went to Florida to visit her mother.

When Tessa's mother saw her in her on the beach in her new suit, she said, "Oh, honey, we can go tomorrow and get you fitted for some nice prostheses." Tessa came indoors from the beach, dropped her wet, salty suit on the floor of the pink bathroom, and left it there. She did not wear it again and didn't even bring it home. When she came home to the group, she told us this story, bewildered.

What might Tessa have said to her mother to lessen the hurt? Could she have told her mother she needed her support, not her direction? Her mother might have recognized that prostheses were an option Tessa had chosen not to take, and that her decision needed to be respected. Could she have told her mother she liked her new body? It's hard to come on strong from the vulnerable position of a "new look," but her mother will have a better chance of responding with care in the future if she knows what Tessa has been valuing and why.

❧

Sometimes words are not necessary. A look, a hug, a touch can mean so much. A smile can carry a load of information. To sit with a sick person and simply hold her hand, and breathe in and out in unison with her, can be more connected, more healing, than any act or word.

I particularly remember finding it hard to speak after an anesthetic. When I did speak, I coughed and felt like throwing up. The nourishment I received from just having my husband sit with me in silence, recognizing that this was all I needed, was the best care possible.

There are many moments when speech is difficult. Yet each of these is an opportunity for being present. When you spend the day with someone in the hospital, it is impossible to talk all day long. Sleep is often the best healer, and to wake and find a loved one still there, reading, napping, is reassuring.

A beautiful healing practice that brings pleasure to both parties is a breathing practice. It is done in silence, using visualization on the part of the caregiver. "Breathe in the pain of the sick person, breathe out the healing energy of the universe": Repeating that image in your mind's eye and continuing it in synchronization with the breath of the ailing person can bring both of you to a place of loving peace. My husband, my daughter, and I sat with my mother as she slept following her hip operation. Together, quietly, we breathed in her pain and breathed out our wishes for her easy recovery. Quietly, as the late afternoon sun filled her room, with the great-grandchildren's pictures looking down on her, we wished her ease and comfort with each breath.

2. Acts of Kindness

The Wise Man never tries to know everything
And therefore he becomes truly wise.
The wise man never acts too hastily
And therefore he finds the best way to act.
The wise man never runs from difficulty
And therefore he finds he rarely runs into difficulty.
                                                    —Lao Tzu

Dear friends ask, "How can I help?" And they truly want to help. They mean it. It is so hard for me, and for many people I've spoken to, to receive help. We are often the ones who give. Seldom sick before this, we are not accustomed to operating at less than full strength. Many of us have no experience of letting people do things for us. But friends are comforted by being able to be helpful, and sometimes we need help. There are many ways to be helpful without being too helpful; many ways to touch the heart of your friend without making him or her feel overwhelmed. There are ways to relieve your need to help without spilling your neediness on to the other person. There are acts of kindness, conversations, and thoughts that can make a difference. The stories in this chapter will illustrate many ways of helping. It is fully sufficient to do *one thing*. The main idea is to do something, not everything, to tailor that act to your friend's needs, and to recognize that simply being with him or her may be more valuable than doing anything

The message I want to pass on is how little it takes to touch people. The smallest act of noticing moves the heart of the receiver. So often in the groups I facilitate, I have heard people say

> What got me through all this was the support of my friends, my loved ones, and my community.
>
> People who I didn't think even noticed me let me know they cared.
>
> The cards and letters meant so much to me.
>
> If someone just asks me how I am doing with this, I feel better.
>
> I believe that I was healed by the people in my community.
>
> I could not have done it alone.
>
> If someone just noted my suffering, I nearly cried.
>
> I never knew I was important to other people.

On the other side of the equation from learning how to give is learning how to receive. There are times in our lives when we need help. It can be a huge gift to allow someone to give, an act that allows the giver, in all his or her helplessness, to feel better. Receiving help can benefit both parties. To allow another to care for us when we need it brings joy into the world while reducing the pain. Opening our hearts to the desire of others to give breaks down the barriers between sick and well, giver and receiver. It is a reciprocal relationship, in which each responds to the other.

The popularity of *Tuesdays with Morrie* lies in our identification with the older man, Morrie. Each of us knows we may someday be as helpless as Morrie at the end of his life, as he dealt with Lou Gehrig's disease. Morrie needed help with every aspect of his life: eating, bathing, going to the toilet, dressing. Morrie accepted and received this help with dignity—and no lessening of his sense of self-worth. He received with grace, as he needed to, and did not feel diminished. He needed help, and people came to him who were pleased to be able to help. There was nothing in his attitude that said, "I don't want people to see me like this. My loss of functioning makes me a less deserving being." He accepted his limitations.

We do not hold lack of physical skills against a child, and children feel little shame, yet when we are declining with age or illness, there is a tendency for us or our loved ones to feel ashamed. It is just a body, and it needs care. I've heard so many stories of people whose lives were enriched by caring for an aging parent. Two women I know became massage therapists after finding the joy in massaging a dying parent. I am sure the parents appreciated the gift too. An exchange of love by any means makes for a kinder world.

❧

If a person close to you becomes ill, do not run away. Trust the relationship you have had to sustain both of you at this hard time. Reach out. It takes so little. I have included below some simple ways we can interact with each other, ways that are undemanding and not overwhelming. Each needs to be tailored to the recipient and to the means of the giver. If you do not know someone well, a card is fine.

❧

When I was twenty-nine years old, with a husband and three children, living in the suburbs of Washington, there was a couple who lived down the street who were even younger than we were and also had three children. Unexpectedly, the husband died. He died unnecessarily. He was given a drug to prevent tuberculosis, which he did not have, and died of his allergy to the drug. I was deeply shaken by this death, although I knew both the husband and the wife just a little. He had sat on our screened porch one summer evening not long before, when a mutual friend had come to town. He was tall, athletic, handsome, and unbearably young. The idea that my young husband could drop dead had never occurred to me, and I could not hold the possibility in my mind for even a full second at a time.

I did not know what to say or to do for the widow. I told myself that I didn't know her well and had no business sticking my nose into her life now, when she would want only her close friends around. I pictured her end of the street, filled with families who were very friendly and engaged with each other, kids in and out of other homes, picnics, parties, evenings with couples together, with and without children. I hid in my house and never called or wrote to her. Luckily, there were some big-hearted women who did live down near my neighbor, and they did support her during those years.

If I had to do it over again, I would write to the young widow to tell her of my sorrow. I would visit her and let her know I was available. From time to time I would take her children on outings with my children. I might drive her places, since she didn't drive. I might pick up groceries for her. I could ask her what she would like me to do.

So I learned. Do something, do anything, or thirty years later you may find yourself writing a book on the subject, still full of regret for not contacting someone in some way.

Years later, I received an offer of help from someone I liked but barely knew, and found out how much this can mean. Shelly told my close friend Laurie to let me know she was available to go with me to appointments or stay with me at home, whatever I might need. I never called upon her, but I felt better for knowing she was aware that I was receiving treatment for cancer and that I could call her.

ॐ

How can you do a good home visit? There are many ways to enter into the daily life of friends without jarring them, demanding they play patient, or patronizing them. I have had friends just get up and do the dishes, no questions asked.

You can, if it is within your nature and the nature of your relationship, do the laundry, clean the fridge, or bring food. If you are comfortable in a friend's house, if you have cooked with him or her, been in and out of the refrigerator on other occasions, then you know the person well enough to do some household chores. If you are less a member of the household, bring in lunch, or let your friend provide food; it is his or her choice. If you are willing to clean the toilet or wash the floor, then you might offer to do that. Stay as long as seems to fit with the condition of the host. It may be a short visit, if she has just had a procedure; longer, if she needs company. Some days, I just did not want to be alone. Friends came and brought a favorite video, and then I did not have to talk; I didn't even have to stay awake. I was comforted by their presence. Read to your friend, if that would please him. Enter consciously; take in the situation. What is going on here? How much socializing can your friend tolerate? Are there a lot of people spending time there, or a few?

If you do not know the person well enough to talk about what he or she needs from you, you might do better sending a card. This is not usually a time for new friends. I found I wanted to see only old friends during the months of treatment; I did not want to put out what it takes to connect to strangers. Sometimes I felt so poorly that I did not want to see anyone but my husband. I knew I was getting better when I enjoyed meeting new people again.

❧

In the arena of helping, it is important to gauge your giving. At the same time that I am a strong advocate for doing something when you hear a friend is ill, I would add that it is important to keep your assistance in line with what's possible for you and respectful of your sick friend's ability and desire to care for himself or herself, as well as congruent with your relationship.

I participated in a program called Being with Dying, led by Joan Halifax, in Santa Fe, New Mexico. In one of the exercises at the program, people worked in pairs, taking turns leading each other around a rolling rocky meadow on a meditation walk. First one person and then the other closed her eyes, gave her arm to her partner, and allowed herself to be led around. When I had my eyes open and was leading my partner, how filled with love and blessing I felt. "I could do this forever," I thought to myself. "This is so gentle and easy. I feel so glad to do this for Amy. She must be so glad she is with me. This is the best in me that is here, now. I will not let her down. I am doing this in such a way that it is easy for her to receive."

When it was my turn to be led, I felt old, stumbling, and stupid. The loss of self-sufficiency was so great that I told myself, "I don't need her; I can find my way with my feet. I can feel, sniff, hear my way around this circle. I feel so sick, so helpless holding on this way. How can I equalize this relationship?" Other people reacted similarly to the two sides of the experience.

When we help, we are in a potentially overpowering position. I try to remember this when deciding how helpful to be. I don't want to make people uncomfortable. I don't want to induce helplessness. I don't want to take away their ability to do things for themselves. At the same time, I do want to do something useful. A balance needs to be struck. As a giver, I sometimes feel helpless. It is hard to remember that my presence is sufficient. I want to rush in and fix and comfort and solve the problem. However, if I am the "fixer," then the sick person may feel broken. Listening closely, questioning, allowing the sick person to set the tone, take the lead, make the plan, is the greatest act of kindness. To take over someone's care is to reduce his or her autonomy and run the risk of being controlling. To engage with the sick person in how he or she wishes to be cared for is an enormous gift.

When a friend offered to come from Vermont to take me to appointments in New York, I felt overwhelmed. But when I mentioned this to my friend Rayna, she didn't have that reaction at all. She liked the idea. I told my friend from Vermont, "Thank you, that's very kind, but I'm sure I can find people here in New York to help out. I will call you if I need you." Rayna would have said, "Great." This is where careful listening and reading of the person with the illness is important. Is she wishing for care, or fearful of care? Is this the time to encourage him to open up to the joys of receiving, or is it a time for him to set the terms of caring?

❧

When Larry volunteered at a hospice program, he was full of compassion and desire to make a difference in the lives of people who are dying. He realized that he wanted to be the one to say the right words to relieve the emotional suffering. He wanted so much to be the one they opened up to about their fears. He wanted to be remembered by them as the one kind face. It took him a year, he said, to realize it was not about his getting it just right. All he needed to do was be there. In silence, in light conversation, in humor, in sadness, in fear, in death, he just needed to be present without his ego getting in the way. It required no special formula of words, just human contact. Real, genuine, understated, with no demands, no expectations. No right, no wrong, no form. Just being. He was taught this, he is fairly sure, in the training program, but it took time for it to become his own.

❧

My friend Alla, who teaches restorative yoga, came to visit during my recovery period. She put me in a relaxed supported posture and let me lie there, stretched but relaxed, soft music playing, for fifteen minutes. Another day she brought over her large box of beading equipment, and we did necklace and earring repairs all morning. Once she arrived with a gooey video, during which I slept and woke, and we were together in a completely undemanding way. These gifts were easy for me to receive. Alla was not putting herself in a position of difficulty, and she was pleasing me.

❧

In Darla's last months, the mothers in her daughter's class organized meals to be delivered to her home about three times a week. Women from other classes heard about the plan, and they too wanted to contribute. Her husband's eyes fill with tears two years later as he talks about those months. He describes how he would leave his office at the end of the day, visit the hospital, and come home to find a delicious hot meal, with enough for another day, ready and waiting for him. He and his daughter would sit together and talk while enjoying this great gift. Sometimes he chatted with the cook of the day, sometimes she just left it on the kitchen stoop. He learned a lot about reheating in those months, and he is still moved by all the time it saved him. He did not have to shop; he did not have to cook. He could just come home and be with his daughter.

&

People asked if they could bring us meals during my first treatment. We lived in Manhattan and could order in any food from any ethnic restaurant any time of day or night. Because when I came home from work, I often had no energy to socialize, I told these people, "No thanks." Later, a friend said that she had learned what to do. "You just take food over and arrive, and there it is, and if company is not welcome, you can leave the food and depart." I thought, "How nice that would have been if I hadn't had to say yes or no but just received." There is something in the saying yes that carries with it a helpless feeling. I have been too trained in self-sufficiency to completely give that up with a cancer diagnosis. My mother taught me to take buses to all my lessons, friends' houses, and athletic events. I was not to ask for a ride. This evolved into generally not expecting others to get me so much as a cup of tea. I had always gotten up to get what I wanted. I learned, during the early weeks of radiation, just how many ways I had of keeping up this do-it-yourself attitude. I did not learn how to say, "Please help me, I need . . ." until years later.

With a friend who is ill, I think long and hard about how I might honor his need to take care of what he can, and how to offer him something extra to ease his day. Food requires lots of questions. Different illnesses bring with them special diets. Many kinds of chemotherapy give people a dry mouth, a sensitive digestive tract, and foods taste entirely different from usual. If I was nauseous after eating a favorite hummus spread, it lost its appeal for months.

Before I had my own treatment for cancer, I wanted to bring food to my friend Bea when she was having chemotherapy. I asked the women in the cancer support group in New York City, which I was facilitating, what they had liked to eat. Many of them liked to eat Jell-O, Popsicles, and Gatorade. Cool, smooth, and refreshing, they go down easily. I made grape Jell-O, bought the other products, and proudly went to visit Bea. I looked, as she unpacked the bag, at all the artificial color that was collecting on her tabletop: purple Jell-O, blue Gatorade, and blue Popsicles. Bea has been a vegetarian and conscious eater for twenty-five years, and I was filling her refrigerator with these poisonous chemicals instead of healthy food. I learned from this the value of asking

What tastes good to you?
What might you enjoy?
How do you get food in the house?
I would like to bring you some food.

I learned to think not only about what I might do to help but also about what I already know about the eating choices of the person I am hoping to help.

❦

My friend Caroline's husband was in the hospital for eight weeks, during which time she visited him daily. She learned during those visits to pause at the door, let go of her own apprehensions about how he would look and feel, and open herself to what her husband needed. She learned to leave behind the rush to get there, the fear that he might have died, the worries she had at her job. She felt a need to enter pleasantly, leaving out her own issues, and she found that by opening herself to his mood, she and her husband often spent the time laughing and unwinding together. It turned out that those were the last weeks of his life. They passed them lovingly connected, relaxed, and enjoying each other. She did not have the stamina to stay with him all day, so she spent afternoons with him, and other people went to visit him in the morning.

Then she was at her best when she and her husband were together. He wanted to believe he would live, there was no need for dread and tribulation, and she helped perpetuate that wish.

Visitors are very important to people in the hospital. I met a man at a meditation retreat and we talked in the bus on the way to the airport. He had a heart attack early one morning and was rushed to the hospital and put in the intensive care unit. He asked a nurse to call his place of work to explain his absence. A man from his workplace arrived a short time later and stayed with him all day, recognizing his colleague's need for a support person in the ICU. Since there was no time to locate a friend, this colleague filled the role.

❧

When Elaine had to go to the Mayo Clinic from Vermont for yet another treatment for her Crohn's disease, Marilyn went with her. Marilyn wanted to make Elaine a priority during her time of treatment, so she rearranged her work schedule and accompanied her friend. Both women were single and worked as freelance journalists; they had met years before when they both worked for the same magazine. Marilyn didn't feel worried about being with Elaine during this difficult time, or about caring for her. She appreciated their relationship and had seen it survive times of trouble as well of joy. Instead, Marilyn was pleased that her life allowed her the time to accompany Elaine to the hospital. Of course, few people are able to do that for a friend: They have children, parents, a spouse, or a job that is hard to leave for extended periods.

Some years ago, when my friend Tamara needed a bone marrow transplant in Seattle, and friends were going out for a week at a time to be with her, I panicked. Would I have the patience, the courage to deal with whatever came up? I had never been with someone in pain. I was terribly concerned that Tamara was facing her own death, and I had no experience whatsoever to bring to my concerns about being with her. I used every rationalization in the book to avoid going. And I was successful. I never went.

Marilyn, however, did not have these fears. She ended up staying at Mayo far longer than the original plan, two weeks instead of five days, due to a complication in Elaine's recovery. On a later occasion, when Marilyn was not able to go with Elaine for another treatment, she was disappointed and nostalgic for the time they had had together. She missed the days of quiet reading and communing with her friend, and the elemental nature of the time at Mayo. The business of living was all that was going on. In those days there arose a deep, easy appreciation for the small moments of life: appreciation for a warm bed, a night's sleep, a friendly smile, an hour without pain. Each moment became so valued that the irritations of ordinary life fell away, and Marilyn felt the intensity and beauty of pure living. To accompany a friend is to enter into that time of essential truth—and even joy.

In my fear, I deprived myself of such a moment with Tamara. In talking to her later about my anxiety and, getting more of a sense of her day-to-day existence during that period, it is clear to me now that had I gone, the Tamara I knew would have been available some of the time, and when she wasn't, I would have just been with her anyway. Our old easy relationship would have shone through to connect us. My fear made her into an object that represented only cancer and pain instead of a person dealing with those things, with the spirit, vitality, and courage that I have come to appreciate.

 è

On New Year's weekend of 2000, large snowfalls were predicted throughout the Northeast. Between chemotherapy treatments, I was visiting my friend Lise in the countryside of Massachusetts. Lise knits. She knits sweaters with seventeen colors and Escherlike overlapping sections. She makes beautiful sweaters that last a lifetime. Lise said she would help me get started on sweaters for my grandchildren, and any time I knit the wool into knots she would untangle it. She went to the store, chose the wool, the needles, and the pattern, and brought them home before the snow began to fall. I had not knit since I was sixteen, when I made a sweater that was so tight I couldn't breathe in it after I forced it down over my head. My mother had been a great knitter, but she died between my third and fourth chemotherapy treatments. The knitting made me feel calm and productive. Lise taught me how to risk ripping out whole rows of stitches and to pick up and go forward. She taught me how to make a neckline that would pass easily over a four-year-old child's head.

The first sweater was a red, blue, and yellow soccer sweater, with a matching hat. For the next sweater, I was so motivated I went to the knitting store with Lise, directly from the chemotherapy floor, and chose a thick bunch wool in deep blue, purple, and fuchsia to knit another sweater for my two-year-old grandchild. This was an enormous gift: the gift of knitting, the gift of sitting quietly, the gift of mourning for my mother while creating.

Perhaps you want to teach a friend to knit or crochet, or you could draw or do crossword puzzles together. You can go to meetings, presentations, lectures, dance, music, political rallies. One man I know, while undergoing treatments for his brain tumor, took tango lessons. Tickets to performance art, ballet, theater, or music are wonderful gifts. Think about what might please your friend, review how you would feel about it, and then do it.

ﷺ

Some people packed up goodie boxes, with tapes, cards, candles, soaps, whatever appealed to them, and sent them to me, and I was moved and delighted. I'm not good at putting together little goodie boxes, and so I was especially pleased by the efforts of these friends. Very simple decisions and actions became harder for me during treatments. Just to open a box and receive was delightful.

There are healing tapes on the market that you can purchase for a sick friend. The narrator leads the listener through a deep relaxation into a healing visualization. You can also make a tape for your friend, in your voice. You can create a short, simple visualization that suggests a place, sound, color, and texture. Ask your friend what would work for her—something very brief and very clear. With soft music playing in the background, talk her through a deep relaxation, and then have her focus on the place, sound, color, or texture that she has chosen. From time to time, interrupt the silence to bring her gently back to the chosen healing image. Stay with the same visualization throughout the exercise. Remind her again, as the mind wanders, to bring it gently back to the point of focus. The whole session can take from ten minutes to thirty minutes.

There are many kinds of gifts that will be appreciated, as many as there are people. The range goes from blood and platelet donations to stuffed animals. Head wraps, fancy gloves, ginger candy, amber jewelry (which is said to be healing), Häagen-Dazs gelato, or hugs can each make a difference. The gift needs to suit the receiver and not be so overwhelming that the sick person is consumed by guilt that he or she cannot reciprocate.

Some friends sent talismans for me to take into treatments with me. A talisman can be any kind of object to which special meaning is attached. It may come from a foreign culture or from childhood, or it may be something that is appealing to the giver of the gift. Some people take these small objects—stones, jewelry, toys—into radiation, or even surgery, with them, as protection. Friends can bless the talisman to give it added significance. Giving a copy of a poem or psalm suits some people, others might want to give teddy bears, bath salts, fancy underwear, jewelry with special powers, healing rocks, or a photo of significance. Some people collect jokes. Lucy had a bag of talismans she took with her each time she went to the hospital.

※

Gifts can take other forms than objects. My friend Claudine bought me an hour's massage with her favorite masseur. Massage, like yoga, can bring one back into a kind relationship to one's body. Often with illness, there is a sense that our bodies have let us down. We may feel withdrawn from our bodies, abandoning the body to do its healing while we are looking the other way. To do gentle exercise, stretching, massage, facials, or to just be touched reminds us that there are many parts of the body that don't hurt, that the body can still be a source of pleasure, and that we do not have to turn away from this aspect of self. Indeed, we need to turn toward the body in order to health.

In the last stage of her cancer, Lucy loved to watch *Survivor* on television. So every week, on that night, a few of her friends gathered in her TV room to watch with her. For the rest of the week, they talked about the last show and predicted what would happen the following week. In this way, when Lucy needed to feel distracted because she was too upset or in pain, there was always *Survivor* to talk about. *Survivor* evoked for Lucy her own feelings of facing a difficult challenge, keeping on with the effort, and surviving.

I find in my groups and with my friends that the spontaneous eruption of laughter is a moment of great well-being. There is no need to think all is doom and gloom. There may be times that a person who has an illness feels it is improper to laugh, but the normality of it, the physical release that comes with the laughter, lightens everyone. Do not hold back lighthearted comments when they arise. When the person who is sick makes jokes, especially, laugh at them.

Laughter is a wonderful antidote for fear and suffering. I remember seeing an A. R. Gurney play called *Sylvia* about an older couple who adopt a dog, played by Sarah Jessica Parker. Watching her shake her long curly hair, run around on hands and feet, and leap into the lap of the husband in the play, I laughed and laughed, feeling like I had come up from underwater, back into the real world for the first time since my diagnosis three weeks before.

My friend Pam keeps a box of funny tapes, videos, and books ready to go out to the next person she hears has an illness. She believes strongly in the Norman Cousins approach to healing through humor. It helps to ask your friend for whom you are choosing humorous material what or whom he or she finds funny. Funny is different for each of us. As I sat and watched the tapes Pam chose for me, I felt as though I was laughing with her by my side, an added bonus.

I have received audiotapes prepared especially for me when I was ill. These tapes, which are easy to make for a friend, can incorporate qualities of your friend that you enjoy and want to draw on in his or her healing effort. Think about what you like about your friend, name that quality, and work it into the tape. Or record a personal message or stories. People sometimes listen to these personal tapes, commercial healing tapes, music tapes, whatever appeals to them, during surgery and report a speedier recovery afterward.

People who are readers want more and more books. Find out what your friend wants to read. If disease research is his thing, send more of that in the beginning, and perhaps later send books that are entertaining or distracting or uplifting. Ask what he is enjoying and send more. Some people want fiction to begin with and books on their illness later.

Arlene read aloud to her mother during the last week of her life. They read Jane Austen, whom both mother and daughter loved. Her mother was barely awake much of the time, but she seemed to be loving the experience of being read to. When at last Arlene and her husband had to leave to fly home, there were only fifteen pages left in the book, and they left instructions with Arlene's dad to be sure to finish it. He finished the book with his wife, and a few days later she died peacefully.

What I would want, if I could no longer read myself, would be to keep a favorite book in my room, and when people got tired of making conversation, they could read to me aloud from the book until they were tired. And then sit quietly with me. The next visitor could take up where they left off. Now I just have to think about what book to choose.

&

It may sound like a small matter, but for a sick person with a pet to know that the pet is being cared for well by a loving friend can bring an enormous amount of relief. Jane picked up Lenny's dog, Lola, every day for months, and walked Lola along with her own dog. This required Jane to go out in her car and pick up Lola and then, Jane being the kind of dog walker she is, take both dogs to wonderful open places to run. Afterward she returned Lola, who plopped down, exhausted, next to Lenny's bed. Jane enjoyed doing this and did not consider it a big deal. But during Lenny's last months, and then at the funeral, Jane couldn't get over the credit she got from Lenny's family for what she regarded as a simple act.

&

There is a great deal of medical information on the Web, far more than most sick people, their minds distracted by the emotional impact of a diagnosis, can absorb. A friend who has the time and capacity to search the Web for useful, accurate information on a disease or condition can be very helpful. Searching on the name of the disease often yields basic information on diagnostic criteria, treatments, and prognosis. Certain sites, such as those of hospitals, well-known treatment centers, and organizations such as the

National Cancer Institute, yield more detailed information on treatments, both common and experimental. Clinical trial listings include the criteria for consideration, the phase of the trial, and the hypothesis that the trial is based on. All these should be reviewed with one's doctor. If a friend or relative is willing to sift through all the data and pass on that which is useful and relevant, that is a great service. Sometimes, on the other hand, "patients" like to do this themselves. It removes the illness from them by one degree and makes them into objective researchers instead of passive victims.

Do bear in mind that there are also many people and groups on the Internet promoting odd, offbeat, unproven methods of treatment that rely on anecdotal evidence for their results. Alternative forms of treatment are available all over the world, and some may work, but they need to be weighed and compared with great care. A good doctor may be able to help you with this. There are also many books available that assess alternative treatments.

&

One woman I know, Janet, creates rituals of transition, celebration, and healing. A group of loving friends, who are open to this rather esoteric form of support, gather by invitation. Together they create a ceremony to uplift, to support, to enlarge the sense of being part of something greater than oneself for the designated receiver. For a healing circle, there could be a center altar that contains pictures of those present, people who were important who have died, children, parents, and spouse. There might be objects from nature, from the life story of the central person, from each person in the room. There could be a chance to talk about what the circle means for each person, what the objects on the altar mean, and what the wishes are from each person. There might be singing, dancing, swaying, praying. Sometimes people bring favorite songs or poems to read or sing together. Meditation is a way to quiet the group and move to a deep state of consciousness before beginning the talking part of the ceremony.

HANDS-ON HEALING

Hands-on healing is very enriching for people who are comfortable with it. The person who is in need lies down in the center of the circle. With lights low and music playing, or the group chanting, the participants hold their hands close to but not touching the person's body. After grounding themselves in an image of the earth and opening themselves to an image of universal healing energy, they each send to the person who is ill all the cumulative healing energy. Many people use a tree as their image, with the roots grounding them and the branches reaching up to the universal spirit. When the person lying down feels ready, he or she raises a finger to let the others know that if they wish to lay hands on, that would be appreciated. For some people, this much contact is not welcome. For others, it is an exquisite experience. Each of us responds in our own way. After the time allotted is over, the person who received all this love needs time to recover, to sit quietly and without conversation until he or she is ready to rejoin the circle.

Churches and synagogues now offer healing services, which many people find supportive and life giving. Services may be dedicated entirely to healing, or in the middle of a regular service there may be a prayer for healing. In synagogues I have attended, people in the congregation are invited to stand together and say, each in turn, the name of the person for whom they wish healing.

❧

Teaching a friend, colleague, relative, or loved one how to meditate is another way of showing care. I offer some general guidance below, but meditation is easier to learn from someone who practices it than by reading a book and simply closing your eyes. It may be hard to learn when the mind is filled with anxiety, and yet meditation is so helpful at such times. My meditation practice and the teachings that support it carried me through many middle-of-the-night moments of anxiety. Meditation instructions are simple; the practice is difficult. But we all know that stress interferes with healing, and studies show that stress is reduced by meditation. Any practice that calms the mind and body and returns us to a place of greater equanimity is worth doing.

Sitting in a comfortable position in an upright chair, both feet flat on the floor, back straight, not touching the back of the chair, head centered on the neck, chin very slightly tucked in, gently close your eyes. Mentally scan the body, from the feet, through the legs, checking the weight of the buttocks on the chair, up through the abdomen, torso, chest, and shoulders, noting the tension or ease of the body as you proceed and come to the head. Note your breathing. Be conscious of every breath in and out. Note when the breath turns around, from in to out. Allow the breath to flow as it needs to: deep and slow, or shallow and quiet. Whatever is happening is just what should be happening. Keep your attention on your breath. When your mind begins to stray, as it will, bring your attention back to your breath, kindly, gently. It is not wrong that it strayed. That is the nature of the mind. No judging, no guilt, just return to your breath. Stay in this position for ten minutes a day the first week, for twenty minutes a day the second week. Keep going. See what happens. Note how you feel just afterward and then later in the day. See what happens after a few days. Know that this is hard to do. To return to the breath even one time in each sitting is valuable.

❧

I had a lump in my groin. I didn't know what it was. The doctor said not to worry, but it didn't feel good to me. I don't like lumps on my body. I touched it through my pants pocket over and over. At night it seemed bigger than in the daytime. I lay in bed and wondered what it was. I got up and read medical books, not knowing what to look under in the index. Lump, lypoma, lymphoma, hernia? None of them told me about my lump and my chances of living past tomorrow. I got back in bed and worried about all the ramifications of illness. Then I would recall the lessons of my meditation: "Everything is impermanent, mind states, physical symptoms, the position of the stars, the tides, the trees, even the rocks. This worry will pass, another will take its place, joy will arise, and joy will pass. Do not become attached to the mind state of the moment, as it will pass. There is nothing wrong with worrying; it is just another mind state. Let it go, gently. Can I do anything about this lump now? No. So go to sleep, Susan, go to sleep."

I did my deep breathing practice of counting to four on the in breath, to five while holding my breath, and to six while breathing out. After several repetitions, I was asleep. Sleep is the great blessing of the day. It is the time of greatest healing. We get out of our own way and the body has time to readjust itself. The body is designed to heal itself, but sometimes it needs a lot of help. I often would wake refreshed.

I had to repeat these phrases regarding worry and impermanence many times, and then the worries relented and went away. Getting a medical diagnosis actually helped, because then many of my questions were answered. Would I live? Yes. Was there a treatment? Yes. How long would it take? How would I feel? Could I work during treatment? Yes. All these questions were answered.

❧

Early in my cancer diagnosis a doctor friend asked, "How can I help?" "Pray for me," I said, and she was startled. No one had ever said that to her before. People saw her as a doctor, not a connection to God. But I meant what I said. I do believe that prayer or positive thoughts make a difference. I loved the idea that people from Israel to Hawaii were thinking of me. When people asked, "How can I help?" I had an answer. They could feel useful, and they were fulfilling my wishes. I felt surrounded by care.

Prayer has different meanings for each of us. For me, prayer is a fervent thought that contains some relationship to God. I believe that focused energy, imagery, and concern can make a difference. There is evidence that prayer does make a difference in healing. Prayers may be said at night before sleep, in the morning upon rising, or at all these times. Sometimes when I think of a sick friend, instead of worrying and tensing up, I will send him or her a prayer. Some of you may call it a positive thought, but nonetheless I send my prayers out with strong intention, focusing on an image of the person well and thriving. Or I send out healing light. Or I may wish him or her a good day. My friend Jerry has a prayer wheel in a stream that is turned by the water, so that all day and all night it is sending out prayers. He lends the prayer wheel the intention of sending prayers to all his friends who are sick, and the prayer wheel does the work, leaving Jerry free to do his work.

There are three kinds of prayer: prayers of gratitude, prayers of supplication (asking for yourself), and prayers of exhortation (prayers on behalf of others). I found that during my initiation into cancer, I was offering up prayers of gratitude for myself, on and off all day. Each day that I felt well, I found myself thanking God for the wonder of that. I had never done this before. A few years ago I prayed hard for a friend who had a stroke. This was different from simply thinking about him. My mind and soul were more engaged; I worked with a very focused image of him, and even if I prayed for only a minute or two at a time, I felt better for it. He feels that the prayers of friends were an important part of his healing process.

I integrate prayer into the groups I lead by ending each session with the members standing in a small tight circle. I might say, "Thanks to the universe that brought us together, that gave us the opportunity to listen to each other and be with each other. I ask that the light in each of us rise up and thrive through the coming week. Let us recognize the special light in the others in the circle, and know that it is in each of us as well, and rejoice in that. May we remember to laugh when happy and cry when sad, and know that each will pass and each will return. Let us draw in the healing energy of the universe and send it round the circle. Amen."

I do not call it "prayer" until I know that people are comfortable with the term. I was teased by one member about my spirituality who later, in our time together, thanked me for introducing her to that aspect of living. She told me it had added meaning and a sense of connection to her life. As she entered into treatment for metastasized breast cancer, four years after we met, she called people and asked them to pray for her. For her, this was a huge shift in attitude, not only toward prayer, but also the value of engaging other people in her journey.

❧

These are many different ways to help people when they are facing an illness. There are so many more I have not suggested here, and part of the pleasure in helping comes from exploring your own creativity. Whether you have known the person for a year or several, how involved you are in his or her life, what you have done together in the past, what you know of him or her all play a part in deciding how you want to give and what to give. I use as my guide how I would feel receiving the offering I am about to make if the I were the sick person instead of the giver. If it feels out of whack, I back off. But if someone is on your mind, it is worth doing something. Small acts of kindness can be deeply meaningful.

What one person is able to receive is often very different from another. Some people grow up expecting to receive, some hope desperately to be given to, and others are taught that it is not "nice" to receive. Fine-tuning by both parties can serve the needs of both the giver and the receiver. Pay attention to what the sick person really wants and cannot do for himself or herself. Or notice what requires a few people to accomplish. Offer what might please you but recognize that it might not suit your friend. Acting from love and compassion can bring beauty into both your lives.

3. Talking to Children About Illness and Death

Loving compassion is like sunlight
Awakening and bringing joy to beings.
Its beauty is like a rainbow,
Lifting the hearts of all who see it.
                    —Jack Kornfield

I found this a difficult chapter to write. I don't like imagining scenes with parents delivering bad news to young children. I cry in movies when parents and children are separated. Books in which parents leave children make me angry. I always remember these books. In a trilogy of books by Doris Lessing, a character named Martha Quest leaves her two children in Africa and goes off to London. She claims they are better off not having a mother to deal with. Thirty years after reading this piece of fiction, I am unhappy when I think about her decision.

I think about Renee, who needed tremendous reassurance throughout her childhood that her mother would be there in the morning. Her mother left on a night-light and repeated stories and reassurance at every bedtime. When Renee was in her twenties, her mother died of breast cancer. Now, at thirty-five,

Renee has been diagnosed with ovarian cancer and faces the possibility of leaving her tiny sons. How can she possibly explain this to them? How can she reassure them, when she is so uncertain of her own future?

It is to the parents with young children, who contract life-threatening illnesses, that I dedicate this chapter. The stories I include here are to initiate you to the complexity of the relationships and reactions in families when faced with serious illness of a parent. The stories are intended to expand your awareness of possible conversations you might want to have with loved ones if you are diagnosed with a life-threatening illness.

This chapter does not address the difficulties of having a child who is seriously ill and how to talk to him or her about that. Thankfully, I have very little experience with this situation so far, and I do not know enough people who have to find my way in this area. Some wonderful books exist on this subject.

❧

When I was eighteen, my mother was diagnosed with breast cancer. I knew she was having a biopsy, and that if they found cancer they would remove her breast. She had explained this to me in a matter-of-fact manner a few days before the operation. I was quite sure it would all be nothing. I went with my friends to my film society weekly showing as usual. Afterward, I went over to the hospital to see what was doing. I found my brother and father alone, in a long, dark, narrow visitors' waiting room. They were just sitting there—not reading or talking. Dad said that my mother had breast cancer, and they had done a radical mastectomy. I did not know what that meant and I was afraid to cut into the silence and ask. I knew I could not go in to see my mother yet; she was still sleeping. My father had never been very communicative with me. We had spent many hours driving around doing errands together on weekends, saying nothing. And here we were again, for a very long thirty minutes, sitting in the waiting room, suffering in silence, all three of us. This is why I now advocate for talking, talking, talking.

&

As parents begin to enter the path of illness, their thoughts and feelings regarding their children run from fear to anger, denial to depression, anxiety to anguish:

How am I going to tell the children about my illness?
I want their lives to continue just the way they were.
How can I help them cope?
How can I not live to see my children walk, dance, marry, and have babies?
I want to watch them grow up. I am afraid to be with them in this condition.
What should I do?
How can I talk to them when I am so afraid?
How can I help them not be afraid?

Do they have to know?
What do I gain by telling them anything?
It is easier for me to bear alone.
I need to protect them from this.
I never thought I would have to do this in all my life.
This was not my plan.

These are typical initial reactions by parents on learning that they have an illness that will require attention over time. Sometimes the children's needs loom larger to parents than their own needs. Responding to one's children in the face of these fears takes planning, preparation, awareness of the ages of the children, and acceptance of one's own limitations. It is an opportunity to offer your children important lessons and skills that will support them through a lifetime. It is a chance to improve your relationship with your children. It can also be a chance to create and add to the precious moments you each will cherish.

☙

Gillian, a child psychotherapist I know, makes a point that parents can do only as well as they are able, given their own innate limitations. If we were all our most mature, self-actualized selves, if we were all capable of managing our own fear so as to not put it on the children, if we all knew how to grieve and could model for our children how to live fully in the face of sadness—that would certainly be the best of all possible worlds. But this is unrealistic. I do think it is important that we try to call forth the best in us for our children's sake. We want them to come through the experience of illness in the family as whole as possible, learning about their own strengths and their ability to deal with what comes into their lives. In the best of all possible worlds, parents would know how to honor their child's way of grieving, letting go, and loving, but I realize that we can each do only what we can do. As with everything else there is to deal with, there needs to be recognition and acceptance that we may not get it just right. Children can live with our imperfect attempt. And there will be, we hope, time to try again, to go back over what we said and see where it needs to be adjusted: There are daily opportunities to apologize for what seemed awkward or upsetting. We need to forgive ourselves for not doing it perfectly. Getting muddled up, not finding the right word, having trouble starting or stopping, this is human. Keep trying. Your most important responsibility as a parent of children who are still at home is to help them deal with their world. It is your job to present the world to your children truthfully, intentionally, and with a desire to help them cope. This is not a time for recriminations and self-abasement. It is a time for softness and self-love. This too can be a lesson for children.

&

From my long experience as a family therapist, I begin with the premise that there is no such thing in a family as a secret. In some way, at some level, secrets are always known. As Wendy Schlessel

Harpham, MD, notes in her book *When a Parent Has Cancer,* social workers report that children know something serious is going on even when nobody says anything to them.

If the facts about an illness are kept secret, the tension of maintaining the secret drains energy from the rest of the relationship. I have never heard an adult say, "I'm so glad my parents protected me from the truth. I couldn't have handled it." I know many who were hurt by secrecy around a parent's illness. Years ago, before Freud and the interest in the unconscious, people felt it was a kindness to pretend to children that nothing bad had happened. The thinking was that if nothing were said, the child would suffer less. In this age of accurately telling people about their diagnosis and prognosis, it follows that children should be given the same respect. Just as we now have open adoption and tell children the truth about "making babies," so too there needs to be truth about illness and the end of life.

ð

In a week-long residential group I cofacilitated on the East Coast, Jeffrey told the group that his father had had cancer and had died of it when he, Jeffrey, was a young boy. The family kept the illness from Jeffrey for so long that he was stunned by his father's seemingly sudden death. If he had been included in the information sharing early in the illness, he would have had time to assimilate the information and, possibly most important, the time to say good-bye. Now in middle age, dealing with his own cancer, he felt he had been denied a role model of how to live with this illness and how to talk about it with his own children. He had to create his own ways. He had to learn from the mistakes of others and try not to follow an example that had been hurtful.

Children are usually aware when there is an elephant in the room that no one is talking about. If there is secrecy surrounding some central issue, it can undermine the entire structure of the relationship between parents and children. Their mutual trust is destroyed. Keeping secrets from children tends to be more detrimental to them than exposing them to hard—even painful—truths.

When you are ill there needs to be plenty of opportunity for your children to ask questions. Many of your questions are the same questions children would ask if they knew how. As you get answers to your questions, pass them on to your children. How you and your caregivers deal with adversity is in evidence every day and will be a model for your family. When the disease is kept a secret, the message is: This problem is too big for you children to handle. Children assume a further message: We do not talk about difficulties in this family, and you should not tell me the truth about what is going on with you when you have a problem. There is a shutdown in communication. This is a great loss at a time when the family could be sharing concern and love. We teach our children how to talk, use the toilet, talk, be with friends and teachers, and we need to get better at teaching them to deal with adversity. To "protect" children from disappointment and difficulty does not prepare them for life's ups and downs. These are opportunities for learning how to care for themselves, which they will need for the rest of their lives.

࿇

When Ann found out she had cancer, she thought for four days about how to talk to her children, and only then did she feel ready. She called them all into the living room after dinner and told her story. She told them how she found the lump under her arm, what tests the doctor performed, and the results. The children were eleven, thirteen, and fifteen. Ann reports that they sensed the seriousness of the occasion and sat tight and quiet in their chairs. They did not know what to say; however, Ann encouraged them to ask their questions over time and assured them that she would answer them as well as she could. She told them that the answers might change from week to week. She told them that she loved them and that she knew they would all get through this. Her children hugged her, the youngest first, and then quickly left the room. In the course of the evening all found an excuse to come to her and curl up next to her on the couch and later on her bed, bringing her their problems of the day and their concerns. "How long will you be sick? Who will make my lunch? Can I come with you to the doctor? Can I see the X-rays?" Through the weeks of waiting for the biopsy results and of decision making, Ann kept the children up to date, as promised, and they appeared to be handling it well. Only when the treatments were over, and she was pronounced "in remission," did the children tell her over and over how tense they had been and how much it had helped for her to talk to them about her cancer.

ॐ

When Leonard was diagnosed with cancer, his children were in high school. He gave a great deal of thought about what to tell them. A writer by trade, he valued words. He knew from his childhood how much words matter at times of crisis. When his own mother found out she had diabetes, he remembers being told that it was his job to watch what she ate. He was about ten at the time and had never done anything in the kitchen but sweep the floor. He had not understood. He was determined to do better for his children. He was quite undone by the news of his illness and spent a few sleepless nights thinking about all he had to do if he was about to die. Mainly he thought about his children, Sally and Frank. He waited several days to get his thoughts in order. What he found was that he grew progressively calmer as the days went by, and finally he felt ready. He called them together in the living room after dinner, turned off the television, and began to tell them from the beginning what was happening to him. He tried to be calm, factual, and caring. When he needed a break, Yvonne, his wife, filled in what her feelings were. Though she was worried, she knew that everything that could be done for Leonard's melanoma would be done.

What Leonard wanted to say to his children included these ideas:

> This is hard to say.
> I think you are able to handle this information.
> Your mom and I are here with you to take care of you.
> We will try to keep your life going on as usual.
> We will answer all your questions.
> Love will help us all to get through this.
> Your mother and I will make the best arrangements for your care that we possibly can.
> Illness affects a whole family, and we need to support one another through this.
> The doctors are going to do everything possible to help us take care of this situation.

He wanted to convey a posture of hope and optimism, a framework that said, We, your parents, can handle this, and we will help you handle it. The information that he gave at the start was brief, and he promised ongoing updates. The children listened closely, and Leonard felt he had done as well as he hoped he would.

ื

Telling your children difficult news requires attention to time and place and their capacity to understand. Surrounding the information with love and care, telling children slowly and sympathetically, reassuring them, encouraging them to come to you not only with questions but also with their sadness and fear, saying that you will deal with this together as a family, allows them to feel included, appreciated, and safe. Children will want to know at some point what the arrangements are for them if you are hospitalized or especially if you die. They need to know this, even if you are going to live for a long time. Children are resilient. Their response to news is shaped not so much by the illness as by how you present it and how well prepared they feel. They get nonverbal messages from you in the way that you present information, and they can sense if you are faking good cheer. If they see you sincerely addressing the facts with hope, even while acknowledging the difficulties, it is easier for them to accept what you say and learn to do the same. It is far different to say, "I'm doing great," when you are not than to say, "I really feel fine now, but I am a little afraid it won't last."

☙

My friend Ram Dass suggests a way to prepare yourself for talking to your children. To help make the talking come from a depth of truth and love, he offers these ideas. He suggests finding a quiet time, choosing the setting with care, and lighting a candle. For the parent who feels uneasy, unsure, or on new ground, a way to move deeply into his or her feelings is to take in three deep breaths and release each one slowly. I would add visualization to this process: Breathe in the calming, healing energy of the universe, breathe out tension and fear. Repeat that at least three times. When the heartbeat of the parent has slowed, and the intention of talking with love to your children has arisen, then real talking will begin. To do this breathing exercise with the child may be a wonderful way to expand the connection to your own feelings. Then, slowly, you can lay a foundation for what may come and instill hope and truth. A few sentences spoken kindly to a child may be all that is needed.

&

I talked with a man whose mother lived throughout his life in a wheelchair; she had polio. While his mother made every effort to attend the plays, presentations, and school events in which he had a role, there was one great difficulty. There was no place in their household to grieve or be unhappy about his mother's illness. No space or time was allowed for sadness. There was no way for a small boy to say, "I wish this wasn't happening to us. I feel awful." No one expressed feelings in this way, no one made room for his feelings, and now, fifty years later, this is what he talks to me about when I tell him I am writing this book. Allowing negative feelings to be expressed is very important. If adults demonstrate for children how they express sadness, fear, or anger, then children will know how to do it when they need to. To express the dark feelings does not make the disease worse, it does not lead to death, and it need not overwhelm others. For a person, child or adult, to say out loud, "I feel terrible about what is happening," releases some of the feelings, allows them to shift if they need to, and often makes the feelings less heavy and more bearable. Allowing children to have their emotions, and to talk about them, is part of the learning process about illness, and it can begin while you are still there to help them.

For both parents and children, it clears the air to express in words the fears, angers, and disappointments that illness gives rise to, rather than acting out. It allows more room for hope, joy, and love. I believe that laughter is healing; I also believe that speaking the truth, crying, and praying are additional ways to heal, and they can pave the way to dying well.

Clear communication can also make recovery more joyful. I think about Rhonda, whose two children were nine and eleven when she and her husband separated and she got the news that she had colon cancer. Rhoda chose an alternative kind of treatment to chemotherapy and was never terribly sick with side effects. She did not want her children to have to bear another moment of discomfort from hearing what was happening to her. I encouraged her to trust her children to be able to handle the fact that she had cancer, but she refused to tell them. Then, at the one-year anniversary of being clear of cancer, she found herself with no one to celebrate with. It seemed too late to tell her kids now, and her husband, who had known, was gone, so the day was outwardly like any other. Inside she both rejoiced and felt desperately lonely.

❧

Children need information to help them prepare to deal with the changes in their world. For example, even after the illness is gone and your treatments are over, you may need rest. This can be explained to children of any age beforehand. Just as we prepare children for doctor appointments, new experiences, treats, and trips, so too they need to be told in advance that you will be away for a day for a treatment, or may be especially tired another day because of a treatment. To come home and find you in bed when you are usually at work is alarming. Let them know in advance what to expect. Then they will be prepared.

&

Jill felt herself regress when she faced a breast cancer diagnosis. A social worker by training, she paid close attention to her children's reactions and noted that they did the same. Just when she felt the need to fall apart, so did her children. Just when Jill hoped that her fourteen-year-old daughter Carolyn would help with some of her extra tasks, Carolyn would retreat into her bedroom, take out an old stuffed animal, and read on her bed for hours. Jill felt angry with Carolyn but knew not to express it, as that was neither fair nor useful. By wishing to regress to an age when her world had been safe, both she and Carolyn were behaving in a predictable, normal manner. Both wished for lost security. Both of them wanted to be protected and cared for, and there was no one to do it.

Jill was able to recognize that these were typical reactions at any stage of an illness and talked to Carolyn about her own feelings, so that Carolyn would have words to understand what she was going through as well. She talked about her wish to have it all go away, the wish for a time when everything was good, a wish to be away from it all. Jill let go of having a tidy house and answering the mail. She was able to arrange for meals to be brought in from outside. Jill felt that talking about her feelings actually relieved her feelings, and she felt that it helped Carolyn deal with her own negative reactions. As Jill calmed down, and let go of having everything perfect, Carolyn came out of her room more frequently to hang out with her mother, talking, cuddling, reading, and laughing.

&

Children may worry that the illness or death of a parent is somehow their fault. Danny's father was sick and Danny went to the fair with his buddies anyway. Danny was only eight and had never gone on such a major outing without a parent. When he came home, his father had died. If he had stayed home, would his father have lived? He has carried this irrational thought to his adulthood years later.

Reassuring children that the illness is fate, that it has nothing to do with them, is important. You might say that you wish it were not in their lives, that you hope to help them deal with it, and that you will try to make life go on for them in an ordinary fashion. Children may also fear that they carry the illness too and will have to deal with it when they grow up. They may fear that a sick parent is going to die when he or she is not. They may fear that no one will care for them. They may worry that the other parent will disappear as well. They may be sad, even deeply depressed. Why is this happening to their family, to them? They may have trouble attending to their schoolwork, and having fun may make them feel guilty. It may feel awkward for children to hang out with friends talking about daily trivia, when at home there is such a life-or-death situation. They may react to this with depression or anger. They may feel that this illness is interfering with their lives. They may feel angry at being less than the center of attention. They may feel held back by a parent's unusual but legitimate needs. They may feel that their life is on hold. They may engage in magical thinking: "If I pray the right way, Father will get better." Then when he does not, they blame themselves. They may make bargains with God: "If I do X, then Y will happen." All these reactions are normal but painful. Talking them through with children helps.

Children's questions are often oblique and not easily recognized as relating to their feelings about your illness. They may ask some question about the future, they may ask about something seemingly unrelated that they saw on television, they may not be able to formulate questions, or they may ask the same questions over and over. Staying aware of children's concerns and confusions may allow you to figure out what they are really worried about. The quiet child may seem easy to deal with, but he or she may be harboring unexpressed pain that burdens him or her until it is revealed.

&

It is important to respond to your child in age-appropriate ways. A three-year-old might be satisfied learning that Mommy has an "owy" and needs to lie down during the day. A five-year-old may want to know what part of the body hurts. A seven-year-old may have heard the names of major illnesses and want to know the name. Whatever the child asks, he needs a truthful answer, with enough content to satisfy him. You will be able to ascertain how much from knowing your child. Think about what you would have wanted to know at his age. Think about secrets that were kept from you and how you felt. A teenager may need to know a great deal. (When I was in training, on the other hand, an adolescent psychiatrist told me that adolescents can hear only telegrams: that is, any message longer than ten words will not be heard.) An adult child may want to hear all the medical ups and downs, or then again, she may not. Adapt your telling to your individual child. Think about the ways you may be giving a subliminal message not to think or ask about your illness. For the child who is distancing himself and running away, put these fears into words, and let him know that when he is ready, you will answer his questions to the best of your ability.

After the attack on the World Trade Center, when caretakers did not know whether or not the parents were coming home, the caretakers had to say something to the children. One caretaker I heard about told the children that Mommy was still on the subway four days later. This was a way for the caretaker to protect herself from the truth, but it did not serve the children well. What children need in time of crisis is not false comfort but reassurance that they will be cared for. They need to know that everything that can be done to find the parent or care for the parent is being done. They need acknowledgment of their own feelings.

❧

If a child is out of town when a parent receives a diagnosis of a serious illness, it is important to get that information to the child at the same time that the other family members hear the news. It is important to tell the child, so she does not learn this fact after siblings or other relatives. The child needs to feel that she is a part of the inner circle, a respected member of the family. It can be the child's choice whether to come home or not, and that needs to be addressed. Often a child will want to come home and yet cannot, because of distance and commitments. There are many ways the family and the child can respond to this situation.

Norah was in Senegal for a semester when her mother, Miriam, was diagnosed with cancer in her thymus gland. Norah wanted to be home with Miriam and her family, but she needed to finish the last three weeks of her classes. Given the time it would take to go home and return so close to the end of the semester, Norah decided to finish the program as planned. Norah realized that she had to deal with her sadness and her fear without her family. She talked to one of the local girls from her class, who took her home for the weekend to the family village. There, she talked to her new friend's mother about her own mother and her fears. The family took her with them to their place of prayer, where they lit a candle for Miriam and sent out prayers for her in their own way. This was an enormous source of comfort to Norah, far away from her loved ones.

When Norah finally did arrive home, Miriam was still very early in her treatment cycle and looked just fine. Many of Norah's worst fears were allayed by reality. There was still plenty of time for Norah to connect with her mother, talk with her about her feelings, and then go on with her life. She felt she had made a difficult decision, one that was the right choice for her.

The ritual and comfort offered to her in a foreign land made Norah realize that powerful healing can take place even with strangers at times of difficulty. Because Miriam had been so open with her, and because Norah had felt confident her mother was giving her the straight story, Norah was able to carry on with her life and studies while she held her mother's situation in the background.

ॐ

One father gave a great deal of thought to preparing his children, ages fifteen, eighteen, and twenty-two, for his approaching death. He did not plan to say all these things at one time, but he had them ready for the times when there was a need for them to be said:

> The doctors and I are working as hard as we can to cure me.
>
> The doctors are working as hard as they can to keep me comfortable.
>
> This is a hard time, and we will do our best to make life normal for you.
>
> I wish this wasn't happening to you, and to me, but we have what it takes to get through this together.
>
> I think you may be frightened, but I know we will still get to have lots of good times together in spite of my illness.
>
> Let's keep talking about what we enjoy during this illness so we can get really good at having great times together.
>
> I feel hopeful that as my illness unfolds we will have what it takes to cope with what comes.
>
> I believe that our love will carry us through.
>
> I love you, and I'm comforted by having you with me in this time.

Over a few days, he spoke his piece to his family, was relieved of his fears, and began to surrender his body to death.

Sometimes when I get difficult news from tests, I wait a week or two before telling my children, even though they are now adults, so that I can have some degree of acceptance about the news myself. I try to share the fact that I was upset by the news and have now calmed down, as a way of modeling what they may go through. After I tell them, I feel so much better. I wonder what kept me from telling them sooner. Sharing the news with loved ones is very comforting and, to me, a relief. Others I know report similar feelings. Just as my family may be helped by seeing that I've accepted difficult news, for me to find that loved ones can handle the disappointment of a relapse reduces my disappointment.

I am also aware that I present the facts very differently on different days, and to different people. In the middle of the night, when I am talking to myself, I am the most negative and fearful. A week later, by the time I tell people I don't know well that I'm having a recurrence, I am upbeat and nonchalant. I can't believe what optimistic news comes out of my mouth sometimes. With people closer to me, when I found out that the lymphoma had recurred so soon after the chemotherapy treatment, I owned up to my disappointment.

I think that a range of responses are needed. I don't want sympathy from strangers, but I do want those closest to me to know what is happening. I have a very hard time telling bad news to people I love. I fear that they will feel sad for a while. Sometimes I have Charlie, my husband, tell the bad news. Sometimes I wait. Sometimes I get up my courage and tell. Then friends say things that are deeply touching to me, and I tear up. At first this was frightening. Now I have come to love those moments of strong feeling. They are so connecting and heartwarming. I feel

I'm participating in the human condition, which includes suffering and letting go of suffering.

≥ε

Remember that you are not alone. There are ways to get through the days of illness and continued work, household chores, and child care. Family members, neighbors, friends, and parents of your children's friends all are out there willing to help. If you cannot handle being the primary emotional support for your children for a time, recognize that there are other people in your child's life who would be pleased to help in this way—a grandparent, a friend, a relative.

If you're the parent of preschool- to high-school-age children and are diagnosed with a serious illness, I suggest that, if possible, you hire someone lighthearted to spend time with your kids. There are many services in large cities for children who are distressed about illness or death. Ask your oncologist, doctor, or nurse. Go online to see what support there is to take some of the burden off you. Especially for single parents who are overburdened even before a diagnosis, outside help is available. There may be nearby family members who are pleased to have time to spend with your children and delight in having a way to be helpful. Though it is a hard time in the life of a person who is sick, to make the welfare of your children a high priority is an enormous expression of love.

Achieving a place of quiet sanctity for healing can be difficult in a house full of children. How quiet can you make the house and still protect your children's need to play? It's hard for young children to play quietly all the time, especially on demand. It's hard never to bring friends home because there is an invalid in the house. Just as you try to keep yourself together for your children, so too do your children try to keep themselves together for you. How do each of you learn, at this difficult time, to express what is true, without being too demanding, without overwhelming each other?

Keep asking, "What is working?"

You may want to arrange ahead of time for noisy playtime and move yourself as far away as possible—headphones, earplugs, and music may help. Recognizing the children's need to pretend that everything is as before, when they came and went and played loud music, may help you to accept this behavior when it occurs even after the diagnosis. Remind yourself that your children, as well as yourself, are living in a time of crisis; this may give you the strength to see them through this adjustment period. It can be helpful to let children know which days are going to be worse or better, if you can. Encourage them to make plans you can participate in on the days you feel better. For the days you are in bed, think up quiet projects that you can do in bed with your children, or games or activities that they can engage in at the foot of your bed, so they can have the pleasure of your company without putting a strain on you.

❧

My mother was very frank about her cancer at a time when most people were not. She told friends and relatives that she had had breast cancer and was now cured. All that was true, and I told my friends the same. But in the middle of the night, the questions started to flap around in my eighteen-year-old mind. Would she die? Would I get this disease and die? When I had a husband, how would he respond if it happened to me? If I had a daughter, would my daughter get it too? What did the scars look like? Were they like the rays of the sun? Could I be strong like my mother? When would I lose a breast?

If I had been given an opportunity to talk about my fears, for myself and for my unborn daughter, it would have been helpful. Seeing my mother's scar would have reduced the imagery that my brain produced. But about this she was very private. Not until my mother was eighty-nine did I get to see the scar. After she had a hip replacement, it was I who wheeled her into a shower room, removed her hospital gown, and washed her aging body. The scar by then was a single thin, curving white line, not jarring or frightening; it just was. Seeing the scar soon after it healed would have been helpful for me, allaying much of my anxiety.

&

When June was nine, both her parents were diagnosed with cancer. The family lived on Long Island and her parents arranged their doctor visits in the city for the same day, at the same hospital. On those days they took June out of school and brought her to the city with them, so that if they were late coming home, she wouldn't have to be home alone. She loved the days in the city. Between or after appointments, they went to the merry-go-round in Central Park, they bought ice cream cones at fancy restaurants, they took rides on the Staten Island Ferry. It felt to June like her day off. She remembers those days with happiness and hope. She felt integrally connected to all they were going through together and felt that she was inside the circle of attention.

Sometimes offering children, especially adolescents, a way to be helpful gives them a sense of engagement, comfort, and security. Simple daily tasks that relieve you and that they enjoy may work well: baking cookies, walking the dog, taking out the garbage. Children may willingly help with light chores. They may even become less demanding of you. Sometimes asking children to take on more responsibility makes them feel valuable. Sometimes, however, they may resent the requests and become more demanding. Just when your strength is at its lowest point, your children's need for you to take care of them may be greatest. When that is the case, back off and try other ways to resolve the issue. The way you deal with these periods and your own depletion will teach your children how to deal with the challenges in their own lives.

In crisis some children feel needed, which children seldom get a chance to feel in everyday life. This does not mean that children should be running households. But some help from them can feel good to both you and them. Meanwhile, they should have the opportunity to check in with their mom or dad about what is truly on their minds and then go on about their lives as they need to.

ᴥ

If you note that your illness is unduly affecting your child, let his or her school know what is going on at home. In children, sadness and fear may be turned into anger and acting out. It is harder to comfort an angry child, but when teachers know the cause of the anger, they are more likely to respond with kindness. When children are depressed, they may become irritable or withdrawn. Keep an eye out for these reactions and help your kids to recognize and talk about what they are truly feeling; this will release some of the tension. Note changes in a child's sleeping or eating patterns, as well as changes in schoolwork and relations with other children. Indicators of underlying emotional trauma often show up in the most ordinary activities. Children who are acting out need limits and kindness, even when it is hardest for you to offer those things.

ᴥ

Preparing children for a parent's dying has special considerations, but introducing children to death need not be scary. The death of distant people, famous people, or family pets is a good place to begin to introduce children to the reality of death and dying. Letting children be involved in the learning process about an illness and about death can be a gift to them. It gives children the message that you know they have the internal strength to meet the situation without being destroyed by it. There are gentle ways to talk to children about the cycles of nature that can help them understand that death comes at the end of life and is inevitable and important.

Darlene raised her two sons in the country, with horses, goats, dogs, and cats around them. She had felt excluded from conversations about death in her own childhood and wanted to treat her sons differently. She encouraged the boys to be present with animals as they died, even when they had to be "put down." Darlene helped her children plan memorials, choose burial grounds, select shrubs for the grave sites, and write eulogies for all the various pets and animals that died while in their care. She feels that her boys learned from these experiences that death is not to be feared. Because of this exposure, she reports, her sons can be with people and animals who are sick or dying without fear or discomfort. When their grandfather was dying, the son who was in town asked to sit with his grandpa during his final hours and to see him after his death. From their early experiences, the boys have become seasoned caregivers.

❧

When Mavis first realized that she needed to be straight with her children about the possibility of her death, she decided to talk to three friends first, before talking to the children. This was very planned and deliberate on her part. She discovered that the more she talked about her approaching death, the easier it became, as had been her hope. Because of the "rehearsals," when it was time to tell her children, she was able to do it in just the way she had wanted to. Do not be surprised by children's silence in the face of these kinds of conversations. We give to our children so they will be able to give to their children. It is enough that they listen to us. It is usually not within their abilities to respond.

One father I know used the car as a container for the difficult conversations he needed to have with his son about his illness. On the way to soccer games and practice, while both father and son looked out the front window, avoiding direct eye contact, the father would explain what early-onset Parkinson's meant in his life and what it might mean for his son. The boy did not have to answer, and he could not avoid hearing. The father could reach over and touch his son when needed, and they could go on quietly after that. The father found that this setting suited him, and he felt that it also suited his son.

❧

When Lana, a single parent, was dying, she put off talking to her son, Steve, until the very last weeks of her life. She was determined to live, and it felt like "giving in" to acknowledge that death could come to her. But her friends encouraged her to talk to him. One night in the hospital, Lana told Steve that she loved him and wished she could be with him forever, but that it was not to be. She assured him that she knew he would continue to be the wonderful young man he already was. She told him who his guardian would be after her death. By now Steve was lying next to her, on the hospital bed, with all of his long, lean seventeen-year-old frame, and they held each other for a long time. That was all that Lana ever said to Steve about her death. On the way home from the hospital that night, Steve repeated his conversation with his mother to his mother's friend Janice. He said he was finally at peace, because he knew that everything was good between him and his mom. It took very few words, just a deep physical connection, to allow each of them to go on, one with living, one with dying.

ॐ

There is a business side to dying. Preparation needs to be made for a will, plans for burial, a guardian for children under eighteen, and the distribution of goods and money. Some people, when facing death, find it helpful to take care of such business early in their dying process. Others may put it off.

When a parent dies, legal guardianship needs to be established for children who are still at home. Close relatives who are passed over for legal guardianship in favor of other relatives or friends need to be told what is planned. Legal papers regarding medical directives for the parent need to be reviewed and finalized. Cemetery plots and caskets can be purchased ahead of time. Plans for the funeral can all be filed at the funeral home of choice so that mourners do not have to make these decisions themselves. The program for the funeral can be planned. The parent can even plan the ceremony with the child, if that suits the child's age and interests.

❧

If you are anticipating your death, your will needs to be in order, reviewed for any changes the years may have wrought, and signed. If you have moved out of state since your wrote your last will, you may need to amend it to comply with state laws. Someone needs to know where you keep your will. If your lawyer has a copy, he or she should be informed during the dying process. There can be statements in wills that reflect your preferences for care at the end of life. Having all the paperwork in order may not only ease the dying process, but it may also be helpful to family and friends who need to make decisions at the end of life.

Ideally, sick people will arrange to have their drawers and closets in reasonable order so that loved ones in the midst of mourning do not have to throw away the accumulation of years. One of the hardest things I ever did was to empty my mother's home of thirty years. "I never know when I might need this," my mother said too often. For some people, however, it is impossible to clean up their belongings before they die. Nor should we have to spend our last months house cleaning. Some people report that closing the house of the deceased was part of the grieving and healing process.

❧

Just as we prepare children for the birth and entry of a new child to the family, so too we can prepare them for the departure of a family member. There are books written for children of different ages. Sharing your own experiences with them is one way to open the conversation. Some parents write their children letters to be opened on future occasions, such as graduations, proms, marriage, and the birth of babies. The letters can reflect the hopes and dreams of the parent for the child and the grandchildren. Some people I know of have written letters of thanks to each child, revealing what that child has meant to the parent. Telling a child what you love about him or her that is unique, and how he or she has enriched your life, can be a blessing. Writing separate letters to each child in the family is also important. You can make a scrapbook for each family member, with pictures of the special times you have spent together. The parent who is dying can make this remembrance, or the parents and children together; even a friend can participate. Think about who in your network of loved ones has the interest and the skills to help in the endeavor and have that person do it. Videos and tapes of the voice can all be dearly loved, lasting treasures. After a parent's death, well-intentioned relatives or friends sometimes remove all pictures of the deceased from the house in an effort to "protect" the child, but most children value pictures of a departed parent. What the child treasures most may be a picture he or she has secretly retained.

Special objects that have belonged to a parent can be given to the child, either before death or after. Books and souvenirs can be passed on as keepsakes. Keep in mind that there are friends and relatives who can help your children remember or find out what you were like at different ages. These people literally carry your history for your children. An interesting idea was given to me recently: Record for your children what experiences in your life made you who you are today and what experiences you wish for them—college, travel, a mentor, a mate. It may be very specific or general, but be sure to tell your children of your fondest wishes for them.

While a slow dying process is difficult, it can be a gift to children when a parent takes a long time to die. It gives children time to get used to the idea and prepare themselves for this eventuality. A lot of grieving can go on even while the parent is still alive and preparing to leave this world. It is not in our power to control the amount of time we have on earth, but if I lie in bed dying a slow death, I will comfort myself with the thought that in certain ways it is easier for my survivors than a fast death. I once worked with a woman whose parents died together suddenly in a car accident, and for years she struggled to make sense of it, to believe it happened, to let go of them. Without seeing them decline and fade, missing the opportunity to say good-bye in any way, she suffered. One psychiatrist I worked with urged a man who was not ill, but was overworking and overeating, to change his lifestyle for the sake of his children, so he would die of old age and slowly, not too soon of a heart attack. His children would have a more manageable loss to deal with than his sudden death, the psychiatrist pointed out, which would not give them the opportunity for reconciliation or good-bye.

❧

I have met several people who lost a parent while young who were "protected" by not being taken to the funeral—and sometimes not even being told that their parent had died. Children's pain of loss is increased by the disregard for their needs at this important moment, their need to have that loss acknowledged and honored. Some people who were excluded speak of having no recall of the months following the death of their parents. And this pain is frequently carried forward into adulthood.

❧

When Alexa was ten, her mother contracted emphysema, but Alexa was never told. Her mother died that same year, and Alexa was not taken to the funeral. When Alexa asked questions about her mother, they were not answered. She and her sisters were cared for by different aunts until her father remarried. Then he collected his three young daughters and brought them to a new home, where they were told that their own mother was not to be mentioned. It felt horrifying and unfair to be left alone after her parent's death. She wants to be sure to do a better job for her children than was done for her. If Alexa had had a family that included her in the grieving ritual, she is convinced, she would be a different person today.

❧

Tara took her son, Sean, with her to the funeral home after his grandmother died. She wanted him to have the opportunity to see his grandmother without life in her, to help him take in the fact of her death. He was interested, even curious. He came into the cold room with Tara, took her hand, and touched his grandmother's forehead. He stood quietly and held his mother's hand. Tara prayed for her mother. When they left the room and went back out to the funeral director, Sean looked up at him and with great seriousness asked if he could please see another body. For Tara, her son's calm and curiosity were a validation of what she had done. She had detoxified death. She had presented it to her son with truth but without arousing fear. This had been her hope in including a nine-year-old in the closing rituals of life.

❧

When Katherine was dying, she wrote out a whole plan for her funeral, including what her children were to wear and what kind of casket she wanted to be buried in. She made lists of her favorite shawls and gave them to the people who had helped her through the end stage of her illness—the manicurist, the massage therapist, the yoga instructor, the wonderful women who gave extra time to the children. Katherine was in her forties and had two preschool-age children. She and her husband were separated. Toward the end, Katherine knew that she was dying, and she did her best to prepare her two small children for this eventuality. She took them in her arms, on either side of the leather recliner in which she spent her days, and quietly told them that Mommy was going to die and would not be here with them in her body anymore. Fear clutching at her throat, she continued to tell them of the arrangements for them and to reassure them that they would be cared for and by whom. She ended by reminding them of her great love for them and her sadness at leaving them.

Two weeks before her death, Katherine rented a wheelchair, called her ex-husband, and had him take her and the boys to the Macy's Thanksgiving parade. Not wanting her kids to miss out on the parade because of her illness, and not wanting to miss their reactions herself, Katherine shared this last great outing with her kids, her cheeks flushed with the cold, her heart filled with joy.

❧

There are excellent therapists and bereavement counselors for children with ill or deceased parents. Large cities may also offer support groups for such kids. Hospitals, doctors, social service agencies, and funeral homes can direct you to the resources in your area. These opportunities for children to speak out their fears and hopes are beneficial for both children and parents. To pretend that an illness is small and will go away teaches children lying, denial, and defeat. To teach the truth, and to teach children to speak openly about hard truths, equips them for a full engagement with life. In a support group, children can express their dark feelings with less worry about upsetting the other people in the room. If they were to do this with other mourners in their family, children sometimes worry, it would make the grief harder for the others. But here, they can hear how other people their own age mourn. They can assess their own coping skills and note how they are dealing with this adversity. Feelings of anger and loss need to have a safe place to be explored; otherwise children may act out these emotions in ways that are destructive to themselves and others.

In a support group for adolescents that I led with one other adult, there were eight students who were thought to be abusing drugs and alcohol. A quiet, depressed-looking teenage girl named Cindy said nothing for weeks. Finally, in a quiet moment, she dared to enter the conversation for the first time. She told us that her mother, age thirty-seven, was dying of colon cancer at home in her bed, and she, Cindy, was the main caregiver. Her father went to work after he laid out the pills for her mother each day. Cindy and her father brought her mother whatever she might need during the day, and then, after school, it was Cindy's job to clean the house, bathe her mother, and make dinner. She was sad and frightened, overwhelmed, and depressed. What happened in the group that day had never happened in the group before, nor had it ever happened to Cindy. She was the center of attention. People became quiet. Tough boys said sweet things to her: "Hey, that's rotten." "God, that's awful." Whatever they said, it was simple and from their hearts, and was an acknowledgment of this girl's deep pain. Cindy opened up to this caring. Color came into her cheeks; she smiled down into her lap. She lifted up her head, and her posture became more confident. After that, people asked about her mother every week. For the first time, she talked openly about her life, both inside and outside of her caretaking responsibility. Relief came in a support group for drug and alcohol users, a strange place for Cindy to deal with the emotions of an adolescent caregiver. But when neither her mother nor her father had the awareness or the capacity to respond to Cindy's pain, she found a place that supported her and cared about her burden.

❧

This morning I talked to Laurel, whose lung cancer is still growing in spite of many treatments. She has learned to treasure the beautiful moments in each day. She has learned to tell her adult children the wonder of living in that awareness. She has tried to teach them that life holds out no promises of how long we have, so each day should be valued. I hear her soft, congested voice over the phone. I feel the love she has for her children, who all gathered with her for Christmas, and who know she may not be with them next year, for what she calls a "family tradition." I know that they are learning from her the wisdom that has come to her from her suffering. This is a gift to your children, I tell her, to have a chance to be with you as you move into this place of quiet loving, appreciation of life, and acceptance of death.

4. Chronic Illness Has Its Own Etiquette

The softest things in the world
May be harder than the hardest.
Soft water can go through the strongest wall.
Knowing this, I know the value of calm.
Knowing this, I know the value of patience.
Knowing this, I know the value of persistence.
                                        —Lao Tzu

On a visit to Russia in 1990, I had the privilege of visiting with two women in their homes in Moscow. I had come through the Jewish Joint Distribution Committee, which delivered food supplies weekly to many frail elderly people in Moscow. Older, Jewish, these two women had suffered through wars, discrimination, and loss. They lived in very similar circumstances. Their grown children had left the country and moved to America. Their husbands had died. They were alone. Their furniture was exactly the same, all provided by the government in the same year, from the same shipment. Weekly, they received staples—flour, sugar, rice, beans, dried fruit, and canned vegetables—from the Joint Distribution Committee. They spoke no English; there was a translator with me the day I visited. But no translator was needed. Their voices, their gestures, their facial expressions told their stories.

The first woman we visited could only lament. "My children left, my husband died. I am all alone. I can't stand my life. I wish I had died when my husband died. I don't know what keep me alive." The food wasn't good enough, and it never came on time. She went on and on.

In a similar apartment, with the same furniture and pictures on the wall, the second woman, who was blind, was seated at a plastic-covered table. She could not thank the delivery person enough. She offered us her hospitality over and over—a cookie, a glass of tea, an apple. She couldn't wait to show us the pictures of her children—she had three grandchildren in Detroit, two in Florida—and to tell us how each of them was doing.

While the circumstances of these two lives were remarkably similar, the two women's responses were very different. One had been born a pessimist, the other an optimist. One felt dissatisfied with life; the other was full of joy. Each responded to suffering in a different way. With the one who was sad for her difficulties, all I could do was commiserate. As for the woman of happiness, it was easy to spend time with her, to hear her story and delight with her in her family.

I tell this story to illustrate that it is who we are, not the illness that may befall us, that informs the way we react to difficulty.

&

What is a chronic illness? When I write about chronic illness, I am distinguishing it from illnesses that have the possibility of going away, and from illness that will bring death in the foreseeable future. Chronic illnesses are those that do not go away, are variable from day to day, do not have cures, and must be endured for the rest of life. They include multiple sclerosis, lupus, Crohn's disease, some heart-related conditions, some cases of polio, paralysis, mental illnesses, allergies, diabetes, back deterioration, nerve deterioration, HIV (at this time), and many others. While often these illnesses are not visible to outsiders, they have a significant impact on the life of the carrier. Often they require a different response from friends than does an acute, life-threatening diagnosis.

❧

It took me six years of living with cancer to realize I had a chronic illness. In the early years of my illness, I wanted to be asked, "How are you? How are you doing? What is doing? How do you feel?" Or, as one friend asked me, "Do you feel as well as you look?" Then I felt truly *seen*. Now I'm tired of the whole story. I just want to go on about my life. I don't want to report the ups and downs of each CAT scan to more than a few people. I have no need for cancer to be part of the conversation. This is a big change from the early years, and it is, I suspect, not unusual for people with chronic illness. The initial diagnosis takes getting used to. Talking about my lymphoma to friends, using the words over and over, made it real. Talking made the idea of cancer more comprehensible to me. I feel differently about the lymphoma on different days, mostly neutral, sometimes fearful, occasionally disappointed, sometimes elated, sometimes proud of my good health, and, once in a while, angry. But now I feel the need to tell only myself how I am. I no longer need to tell others, nor do I care if no one asks.

か

My friend Dave, who lives in a wheelchair, has talked to me about how caregivers want to fulfill their role as helpers and so demand helplessness from him. They want him to stay in his role as receiver of their largesse. But Dave wants to do what he can for himself. He feels that people want to make decisions for him that he is capable of making. He wants to be seen as a competent person, not a patient.

Some people who suffer from chronic illness only want to pass for ordinary. Some want special attention. Others want only their closest friends to attend to them. The particular person and the relationship dictates what words and actions are appropriate. The stories below may help to inform your choices.

か

Lila, a young woman in her thirties, wants a different response than some other people who have lived with their conditions for a long time. Diagnosed with a benign brain tumor weeks after her first child was born, she was warned of the possible hazards from the operation. And indeed, they all came to pass. A nerve to a major muscle on one side of her face was severed, and she lost the hearing in one ear; her balance is disturbed, her smile is one-sided, one eye does not blink or close for sleep. Her whole facial repertoire of movement is radically different. She looks odd. But no one asks, "What has happened?" Most of her friends have not said, "I am so sorry this is happening to you."

Because Lila's facial responses to situations are asymmetrical, they cannot be read accurately by others, and this interferes with communication. She perceives a degree of misunderstanding because the usual clues are not there.

Lila wants sympathy. Without acknowledgment of the change in her, she feels isolated with her problem. Her husband and child have been enormously sustaining. And there are a few friends who know to say, "I am praying for you," "I am thinking about you," and "I hope there is some improvement over time." Perhaps because people know it is a long-term problem, perhaps out of fear of hurting Lila's feelings, most are afraid to say anything. But the result is that she feels unseen and not cared for.

Lila would not mind if strangers asked her questions. "It's hard to have to explain without being asked," she says. It would help her if people asked her, may I ask you how this happened? Does that hurt? Do you mind if I ask you about your face?" She finally told a few coworkers about her condition and then asked them to spread the word.

Lately she has had some nerve regeneration. For Lila, every new twitch is a cause for celebration. She would like to celebrate these improvements out loud with her friends and colleagues, but she feels her friends are not open to this. They are not able to talk about her losses or her gains. She is lonely.

❧

When Ellen was sixty-five, she developed fibromyalgia. A doctor herself, she knew that the prognosis was not good. She had been a swimmer and hiker all her life, and she was unable to imagine how she would deal with this condition. But she did not want to talk about it with her friends. She told people she was facing this change in her life, but that was all she wanted to say. She didn't want the conversations with her family and friends to be about this situation; she didn't want advice or to hear people "moaning and groaning" about her, as she put it. Instead, she wanted to try to live a "normal life." From the time of diagnosis she took this stance. It was knowing that fibromyalgia would be with her for the rest of her life that dictated this response to her; if it were a curable or treatable condition, she thought she might feel differently. Then she would want people cheering her on. But with the long-term nature of fibromyalgia, she didn't want the disease to be fore-ground in her relationships, or in her consciousness.

❧

When Patrick, a college basketball star, was only thirty-two, he had a stroke. This left him with a limited range of motion in his leg and arm on the left side, and an asymmetry in his face. He was deeply fearful of having another stroke and dying. He told only his father and his wife about his condition. But he didn't want friends to know; he hoped that no one would ask. The way he acted let most people understand that he was not open to conversation about his limitations or illness. People in our culture have been taught not to talk about physical differences, and so his wishes were respected, mostly. But he had not thought about his three-year-old nephew, Steven. He had forgotten the honesty of children. Steven climbed up in Patrick's lap one day and began to touch the stroked side of his uncle's face.

"Poor Uncle Patrick," he said. "Uncle Patrick has an owy." Patrick felt his armor soften in that moment; he felt his need for human compassion arise, and he did not correct Steven. He hugged him, and thanked him, and asked him to touch him more. "It makes the hurt go away," he told his nephew.

Patrick had a dream that night, in which many of his friends appeared. Patrick was in a wheelchair, but nobody mentioned that. They were all busy building a car together. In the following days, Patrick began to rethink his privacy issue and to introduce his stroke into conversation. His friends responded in ways that let him know how much they had wanted to be able to give love, attention, sympathy, and concern. To hold so tightly to his pain had denied them meaningful contact with him.

❧

Matt has a long-term kidney disease. He is currently awaiting a kidney transplant. In the meantime, he must receive kidney dialysis four times a week. It takes half a day each time, with travel and rest. Friends and relatives take turns going with Matt. He says he does not need this care, but he does like to have someone with him. It has been hard for Matt to learn to accept that he needs help; this has been the hardest part of his illness. He likes it when the assistance is given quietly, without insistence. He has a friend who calls occasionally and says, "I have some time today. I'd like to be with you. What's happening with you today?" And then the friend finds a way to fit into what Matt needs that day.

★

Charlene has multiple sclerosis and has been confined to a wheelchair for the latter part of her life. When asked how she is, she says quietly, "I am doing as well as I can, thank you." There is something in the way she greets me each time we meet that keeps me from uttering words of sympathy. One day I asked her what she was thinking when people asked about her health. When people speak to her as a sick person, Charlene said, she feels they are saying, "You are sick; I am well. I'm not going to get what you have. May I never get what you have. How can you bear it?" She dislikes this feeling, and so she does her best to keep people connected to the aspects of her functioning that are well. Instead, she says, she would not mind being asked, "Do you want me to ask you how you are?"

❧

Angela, who lives with a kidney disease, is reactive to the question, "You're fine, aren't you?" She is not alone. Others join her in this dislike. The question, when formulated that way, allows for one answer only. "Yes. I'm fine." It implies, "Say you are fine; that is all I can hear." Angela then feels she has to fix the other person's fears. The closed question allows for only the one answer the asker can bear. It does not allow the truth to come forth.

People seem to need to tell her, "You look wonderful," even though her color is off and her face is strained. Her friends become difficult for her in these moments. She wishes they did not need to comfort themselves in this way. When people ask how she is, Angela usually responds, "Hanging in there." Angela feels that keeps the conversation short. It conveys two messages: "Don't ask" and "I am not all right." This is the truth.

❧

Ernst has lupus. He was diagnosed eight years ago when he was in his fifties. Ernst is more than six feet tall, handsome, and athletic. He does not look as if he has an illness. His face is relaxed, he smiles easily, and he radiates pleasure in life. But he, like Lila, notes his losses. He loved to sail, to hike, to be outdoors. Now he tires easily, his muscles are very weak, his joints ache, and his lungs and breathing are starting to be involved in the decline. For a while Ernst explained lupus to his friends, since few people know much about it, and the disease affects people in many different ways. Now he is tired of the conversation, and he doesn't bother explaining. People have stopped asking him about his health unless he is hospitalized, as he was this winter. He suspects that people think it is all in his head, that he is a hypochondriac. He likes being asked, "How are you?" Often, lately, he finds himself making jokes, light remarks in response to the question. But he still likes to be asked, or just to have someone say, "I'm thinking about your health problems." Just a word that acknowledges that he has an illness and that he suffers.

☙

Even after thirty-five years of living with a life-threatening illness, Maya does not know how to answer the question, "How are you." Maya, now fifty-five, has been physically handicapped since her midtwenties. The hardest part for Maya was the early years, when she was not feeling well and there was no diagnosis. Rounds of tests, uncertainty, and discomfort made her fear she was crazy or psychosomatic, or that the symptoms were about to go away. Finally it was determined that she has an autoimmune disease. Much less was known about autoimmune diseases thirty years ago than today. Her constantly changing symptoms led to difficult treatments.

After years of her illness, people don't ask about it much

anymore. And Maya has never wanted to explain much, except to Justin, her husband. She prefers her friends not to check in on her. She has learned how to stop the questions. In response to the questions that do come, her internal voice answers, "I feel terrible. I want you to feel as angry and terrible as I feel." But she recognizes the good intentions of her friends and does not say these thoughts out loud. She understands they need to feel they would handle the disease as well as Maya appears to. She feels their needs. She has learned to answer, "Thanks for asking. I'm okay."

❧

Katie went to the movies one night, and as she moved into her seat, an old friend stood up three rows back and shouted to her, over the heads of other members of the audience, "You're okay now, aren't you?" Katie responded with the "right answer": "Yes." To say anything more at that moment was not possible. She felt his need to be reassured. She didn't want to interfere with his evening by saying the truth: She had just learned that her stomach pains were from colitis. She answered her friend as he wanted to be answered. She recognized that he cared but was frightened to hear bad news.

In general, Katie has discovered, just a small word or smile can reassure the person who is asking after her. And it's worth her while to move him or her gently into the mode she appreciates. When she likes the person asking, and it's in a less public setting than a movie theater, just by lightening her tone and expressing some brief truth of how well she is handling her situation, she can get back from friends the kind of response she likes.

When Katie was in the hospital, an old friend, Mark, came to visit. Mark had always been extremely awkward, but Katie actually loved this quality in her friend. He entered her hospital room mumbling and shaking his head. But Katie was so happy to see him that she moved easily into the voice and manner she had always used to engage Mark. He immediately picked up the cue from her that she was still Katie, and he responded to her in kind. She got back the Mark she has always enjoyed, he lost his shuffle, and they had a great visit. It was worth it for Katie to give two seconds of attention to easing Mark into the visit. They both benefited.

❧

Injured when young, Anthony was using a wheelchair full-time by his twenties. He lived on his own, in a specially designed apartment, and he had a special van with a lift for his chair, but there were moments he needed help, especially when he arrived at a destination and had to get himself from his car seat onto his chair. The first several times he went out on his own, he sat in his car looking angry until someone noticed the wheelchair on the platform and asked him if he or she could help. Then he went home for Thanksgiving. Anthony has three large older brothers. He told them he was trying hard to take care of himself and that it meant a great deal to him to be able to do so. The brothers, without consulting each other, all separately expressed their frustration at Anthony for not wanting their help. They told him how hard it was for them to watch and do nothing. Listening to them, he came to understand what he would feel like in their place. He realized that he needed help and that others liked to help him. He learned to lean out of his car window and, in a neutral, undemanding way, ask passersby if they would help him for a minute. Someone always does.

ð

At fifty, Ginger realized that she had lived with multiple sclerosis, of the recurring, remitting kind, for half her life. In that time how she would like to be treated has shifted. At all times, she wanted to be seen as a whole person, with a condition whose symptoms come and go. She is now brief and truthful in her answer to the question, "How are you?" Sometimes she answers that she is having a tough spell and leaves it at that. If people ask for more, she responds. What gives her pause is when friends call and leave a message and expect an immediate response. Sometimes she has symptoms that keep her from answering immediately. A few friends have become angry with her, though she has tried to explain to them that she is not always in a state to respond. For people with a chronic illness, it seems to me, the usual rules for calling back should be suspended.

At twenty-seven, when she was first diagnosed, Ginger felt like a failure. Her boyfriend left her; he didn't want to care for her. Her parents and sisters were shaken. She felt ashamed and was very private about her diagnosis. Over the years, as she and her friends matured, she felt ready for the openness she now exhibits.

Ginger began to like having people ask. She felt they were taking in the reality of her life and acknowledging her struggle to stay strong. She doesn't want to be seen as "sick," but she doesn't want to deny that something is going on in her body, either. She finds that when she talks about how she feels, there is a release. She is no longer carrying the burden all alone.

&

I went to the Plush Room at the York Hotel in San Francisco one night to hear my favorite cabaret singer, Andrea Marcovicci. Beautiful and brilliant, a performer, singer, and dancer, she appears to be at ease both when singing and when strolling through the audience engaging with her fans. The man behind me was wearing a neck brace. She asked him, with curiosity and candor, "Is that short- or long-term?" "Long term," he said and beamed at her. Then she said, "I hope the other guy looks worse off than you do." He laughed and reached out for her hand. The acknowledgment, the recognition that he was enduring something, meant a great deal to him. Her light, easy comment and the depth of his response reinforced that many people do not mind their condition being acknowledged in a neutral, interested, nonalarmist, or in this case, humorous way.

&

As I went off to lunch with one friend recently, I wondered about her chronic, intermittently disabling condition. How could I sound sympathetic but not make her feel separate and sickly? What did she need from me? What did I need for my comfort level? How could I offer her respect? Her needs had to come first: her right to pass as ordinary, or to be acknowledged as someone dealing with a challenge. What would she like? I might say to her:

I am thinking about your condition.
Do you want me to ask you how you are today?
How often do you want me to ask?
What is hard for you when people react to your situation?

There are lots of people with chronic illness I never check in on like this. It depends on how well I know them. Am I ignoring the suffering that they endure, or paying too much attention? In the end, the relationship is what defines my level of engagement. What I find is that I check in with people somewhat more often when they are ill than when they are well.

æ

Penny and her two children moved to Texas with her firm when it relocated. She had suffered from chronic back pain for many years and continued to work. In the new community, she wanted not to be known as the "bad back lady"; she didn't want her condition to be known to her new colleagues. She shouldered her pain with her customary strength and built a new life. A year after her arrival, a colleague ran into her in the waiting room of her orthopedist and expressed his surprise. "You don't seem like someone who has always had a bad back," he said. "You seem like an active, productive person." Penny loved this comment. This had been her goal.

❧

Andrew learned in midlife, just after a promotion and the birth of his second child, that he had Lou Gehrig's disease. He tried hard to go on about his life, facing each day as it came. When a friend heard what Andrew was dealing with, he said, "I know you and your strengths, and they are shining more than ever these days." Andrew was renewed in his efforts.

❧

Cynthia, who was chronically ill, was at an ordinary PTA meeting when a neighbor she hardly knew came up to her and said, "I scarcely know you, but I heard about your condition. I so admire your vitality in the face of this."

❧

Daniel's boss, a man he had always admired, came to Daniel years after Daniel told him about his chronic hip pain and said, "If I ever have to face what you are facing, you will be a model to me."

❧

Caregivers often like to be asked how they're doing as well. This is true with acute as well as chronic illnesses. The people who are most engaged with the person with the illness have issues of their own. Fear, sadness, a sense of responsibility for bearing more than their share all play a part in their everyday life. They, sometimes more than the person dealing with the illness, need to be asked

How are you doing?
I think about the complications of your life.
Any time you want to talk, I would be glad to listen.
I see all you do to keep you both going.
I see your life is changed by this too.
Please let me know if you need my help.

There comes a point for people with an illness where they don't want to explain yet again the nature of the disease and the treatment. This is a useful role for the spouse or primary caregiver.

About a year after Stan had a stoma inserted into his windpipe, through which he breathes and talks, he and Verona went on a cruise. For the first year after the surgery, he saw mostly his old friends, who quickly became used to the way Stan now spoke. He sounds husky when he speaks, as though he has a bad cold. He and his wife had not thought much about spending time with strangers until they were on board the ship and eating meals three times a day with people who did not know quite what to say or do. Stan has a wonderful sense of humor, and he quickly learned that if he talked a little about this apparatus and how it came into his life, people were put at their ease and came to accept him easily.

Verona found that she too could speak for Stan and tell his story. She learned to recognize when people wanted to talk to her about Stan while he was not around, and she was able to tell them about Stan's cancer and how his stoma worked. She was happy to do this for him. They both reported that people in general were kind and accepting of this unusual disability.

An odd side effect of Stan's stoma, and one that must happen for a lot of caregivers, was that Verona was treated as "Wife of Stoma," not as a person in her own right. But one woman went out of her way to inquire into Verona's own work. Verona is an academic with years of experience, credits, and publications, and she has broad interests. She likes to talk about whatever she is currently researching. On the boat, the woman who had been interested in who Verona is in her own right became a dear friend.

ॐ

People with AIDS, or other infectious diseases, face particular problems in our culture. People are often curious how someone got the disease; with HIV and AIDS, particularly, they may want to know if it was contracted through sex or drug use. This is nobody's business. To ask, "How did you get this?" is not appropriate. Similarly, there are very few of us who know what caused our cancer or chronic illnesses. Whatever we did, millions of other people do without getting sick. I know so many women who have been on vegetarian organic diets for twenty years, for example, and still got breast cancer. The question has many layers to it. "What did you do that I should stop doing? What did you do that you can now feel guilty about? Please reassure me that this will not happen to me."

All of these assumptions reside in this question. It's a question we can drop from our repertoire.

෨

Henry had herpes. He took care to use protection when he had sex, but in relationships he found it necessary to tell the truth. It was hard to get started, hard to jump into this arena. He had to make his own opening each time. "I have to tell you this now, or I never will." He found that if he told his story with some trepidation and yet expectation of acceptance, it went well. Eventually, Henry met the woman of his dreams and married her.

෨

When Jed, who was HIV positive, was cutting up some salad in his friend Keith's kitchen, he cut himself with a knife. Not a deep cut, but nonetheless, blood welled up at the knife line on his finger. Jed said calmly, "Please let me take care of this. Bring me a bandage, and I'll cover the cut and wash up after myself." Jed bandaged himself, washed the counter, and threw away the sponge. Keith appreciated that Jed handled the situation so matter-of-factly.

෨

Chronic mental illness carries its own set of considerations, including the stigma still attached to such conditions. Thomas had always experienced pronounced ups and downs in his moods, but on turning sixty he experienced a depression so deep that couldn't get out of bed. He called over and over for his wife, from whom he usually asked for very little. Eventually, he began to talk about suicide. It seemed like the only way out. His wife, who hid his state from the world for a few weeks, realized that she needed help and called his doctor. Thomas was hospitalized with twenty-four-hour supervision. Thomas had a very high-status, visible political appointment, and it was important that his condition not become public. There was tremendous pressure on him to "get better" and go back to work.

In the hospital, Thomas was put on medication and underwent electroshock therapy. Still, it took eight weeks for him to begin to experience a shift in his ability to function. He didn't know how to handle people's questions, or what he wanted to tell his children. It was all too much for him.

As much as his wife wanted to respect his wishes, it fell on her to figure out what to do. She was very open with the children, who were in their twenties, and told them the truth. They visited their father in the hospital and let him know they cared. With people from work, and even with their friends, it was much more difficult to decide what to say. After discussing the possibilities with her parents, she decided to write set statements for different groups of people. With close friends, she described her experience of what was happening, offering hope for Thomas and a request for support for both of them. With Thomas's colleagues, she said only that Thomas was unwell and was taking a few months off. Thomas was able early on to call his work and arrange for a leave of absence. He told only the person in charge of absentee arrangements some of what he was experiencing and asked for confidentiality for his situation. This request was met. On Thomas's return to work, people quickly picked up that he didn't want to talk about where he had been, and they respected his wishes.

෬

How to respond to a person suffering from a mental illness is a difficult area. Again, I come back to how well I know the person. Depression is more of a secret than lupus or cancer. It is very hushed. There is such a deep implication that it is the fault of the sufferers. Why do they not just keep going, sooner, better, faster? Who can ask and what to ask is completely dependent on the relationship and the way the person with the condition carries it. When I have called my friends while they are in the hospital, it is important that I ask, "How is it going today?" in a brief, neutral sort of way, leaving an opening for the briefest or the longest of answers. Or just, "I am sorry you are going through this," is sufficient. I find myself biting my tongue, trying not to fling out solutions: exercise, diet, meditation, showers, flowers, manicures, dogs, and birds. It is nearly unbearable for me just to listen and not try to resolve this unendurable impasse. But depression and, indeed, all mental or emotional problems, is not going to be solved by a telephone call with a friend. The very nature of these tenacious maladies makes them sometimes harder to treat than cancer.

I have a friend, a psychotherapist, who had sat with many other people through their depression, yet who became so seriously impaired by the immovability of his own depression that he could not work. Indeed, he found it hard to go to as public a place as a supermarket. It was not my job to suggest meditation and the other 599 ideas I had. It was hard to know what to do. I tried to say, "I'm sorry this is happening." I called, so he would know I had not forgotten him. I wished I could do more. After the depression lifted, I asked him if the calls mattered to him. He said that although he was not able to return calls, he was glad to know I had called. It helped him to know he would have friends to be with, when he was ready.

ह

Margaret has very different desires from Thomas regarding her mental illness. She recognizes that there is a stigma to having a mental illness, but she does not wish to be trapped by that. She wants to talk about her illness, her symptoms, and what her experiences are. She wants to be asked and to be attended to by friends and loved ones. She is very engaged with her world. Recognizing that others have difficulty with mental illnesses, Margaret still hopes that in her circle people will learn to ask her about her illness and how she is doing. She will teach them, she says. She is an expert in manic depression and likes to talk about it. The people she is most appreciative of these days are her aunt, her sister, and her brother, who have dared to ask and to listen. Her brother, though not intimate with the language of emotions, comes first to visit her when she is in the hospital.

Margaret says that some people, on learning that she has a mental illness and is on medication to manage that condition, move away from her. Yet she does not want to hide from them an important facct of her life. She hopes that people will learn that mental or emotional difficulties are not to be shunned. They are not contagious.

Margaret doesn't talk much about her manic depression at work. Her boss, who knows, seems to treat her with kid gloves. She wishes he wouldn't. She can handle her job. If she is late, it doesn't mean she is depressed; it means she overslept. Over-solicitousness can be a burden. So can people using words flippantly in conversation that carry meaning for her: "depressed," "crazy," "manic." This feels like a trivialization of her problems. "Depressed" is not what you feel when you can't find the kind of orange juice you want at the supermarket.

&

When Lester and his son Case visited Lester's father, the nursing aide was busy, and it fell to Lester to change his father's diaper. His father said, as any of us would, "I hate for you to have to do this for me." Lester responded, "You changed my diaper; I want to change yours. I changed Case's diaper, and someday he will change mine. That's just the way it works." His father relaxed and accepted it.

When my own father was in a nursing home, because my mother couldn't care for him at home, my sons came to visit him from their far-off cities. Dad was eighty-five, Phil was thirty-one, and my younger son, Bob, was twenty-seven. Dad needed a shave. Phil shaved my father, and Bob shaved the man who shared his room. I don't know where the person was who usually did this for the gentlemen, but for my sons it was a significant act of caring and of connecting to the process of aging. How different Dad's skin felt from Phil's skin. Someday, each of them will need this care, have this kind of furrowed cheek. I saw their gentleness as they cleaned up the two men and delighted in their generosity.

❧

At first Mattie's mother resisted the idea of a foot massage. She had never had one in her life, and she did want to trouble anyone. But Mattie offered a few times, and one day when she came with some oil, her mother relented. Quietly, calmly, Mattie gave her mother the first foot massage of her life, and her mother loved it. It became an easy favor for Mattie to do for her mother.

Later, Mattie learned that often at dusk her mother began to lose contact with reality. She would retreat into memory and dreams. When Mattie was visiting, just holding her mother's hand while they were sitting together chatting seemed to help ground her mother and bring her back into the present moment.

❧

With older people, and people with Alzheimer's disease, the past is often more with them than the present. Answering questions about their current situation may be impossible, but they will remember every detail of a story from childhood. There are fabulous tales all waiting to come out. Just ask the question.

What did you love when you were six?
What was the worst day you ever had at school?
Who was your first friend?
What did you do in the summer?
When did you first see the ocean?
What kind of adventures have you had?
What was your favorite toy?
Do you have a photo album we can look at?
How did you meet your spouse?
Can you remember your first kiss?
Which of your jobs was the best? Why?
If you could be any age, what would it be?
If you could live anywhere for a year, where would it be?
What would you change if you could?

❧

I am often reminded by people with long-term illnesses of the burdens that occur when friends do too much. This is a tricky area. The overdoer is not afraid to reach out; she does not weigh her action and try to determine if it fits her life, the relationship, the ability to receive and the needs of the sick person. The overdoer is the person who says, "I can fly to your city to take you to your regular doctor's appointment." The friend who insists on driving when the disabled one is insistent that he wishes to take a bus is an overdoer. My fear is that overdoers are not able to look accurately at their own helpfulness, so I put in a cautionary word: A little response to chronic illness goes a long way. Even a little help may be too much. Another way to check in to see if you are giving too much is to think about your internal experience. If you are feeling like the one person on earth who can be helpful, and who can do it best, you are possibly overdoing.

If you are sick, it's important when you are feeling overwhelmed by someone's helpfulness to speak about it. Just saying, "That offer is too helpful to me. It is more than I am comfortable with," can clear the air. If you do not say what is too much for you, then how will others learn to treat you as you wish to be treated? Giving feedback is another way of expressing your needs. When you state with care, "This is what I need now," there is little likelihood of hurt feelings.

On the other side, it is also important to say, "Thank you," when you have received care or attention. Caregivers need feedback and reinforcement to help them find the way to interact with you without guilt and confusion. They need to know they have pleased you. It may seem that this doesn't need to be said, but I've heard of occasions in which the care was treated as an expectation, not a gift. "Thank you" goes a long way.

ॐ

Amanda has lived with Crohn's disease for years. In midlife, her friend Michelle was diagnosed with ulcerative colitis. Amanda, with the best intentions, called Michelle weekly to check in on her. But the calls turned into an interview. Are you doing this, that, and the next thing? Amanda would ask, until Michelle stopped answering her phone. All Amanda had to do was ask, "How's it going?" and listen to the answers. It was difficult for Amanda not to offer advice; she had found some alternative treatments helpful to her, and she wanted very badly for Michelle to undertake them. But these treatments did not suit Michelle. She finally said to Amanda, "I need you to check in on me less." Amanda said, "Oh, okay," and quieted down.

ॐ

When Ray's friend Edgar was diagnosed with Epstein-Barr disease, Ray wanted very badly to help. He called Edgar and asked what he could do. The men lived on opposite sides of the country. Edgar asked Ray to e-mail him every so often; he found that an easy and comforting way to connect with friends. Ray was anxious to please. Either he did not hear Edgar, or that was not enough for him. He asked again, "How can I be helpful?" Edgar, to keep things simple, repeated his wish, "Please e-mail me." Ray, one more time in the conversation, asked his question. Edgar said, "I will let you know," and got off the phone struggling with irritation. He had given an answer, but it was not enough. It had not worked. What was he to do? He shrugged and went back to his desk. He did not have energy for this dance. He was fond of Ray and did not want to make Ray look at what had just gone on. He just wished that Ray could have listened.

&

Ginger has lived with multiple sclerosis for years. She is from time to time slowed down, but she maintains her optimism in spite of her condition. A point of etiquette that Ginger raised is that sometimes friends have given her name to a stranger with MS to call and talk to her, without asking her first if she has the time, interest, or ability at the moment to do that for someone else. They do not stop to consider how needy the stranger may be. She wishes they would ask her permission to do this. Some days she is well enough to respond, but some days she can only just take care of herself.

&

On the other side of the equation, there are sick people who ask for more than can comfortably be given. If, as a receiver, you realize that you frequently feel unloved and abandoned because of a refusal of aid, you may be setting up tests of whether you are loved or not rather than just asking for help. As a giver, it is all right to tell a person with an illness who asks for more than you can give, "No, I can't pick you up in San Raphael, drive you to Berkeley to buy shoes, and take you back to San Raphael, when I live in Berkeley. But I can take you to buy shoes in your town." The caregiver needs to protect his or her health as well.

A clean request for help because you need it, and a clean statement of how much help you can give, are the ways to keep openness and honesty in the relationship.

ૐ

As I approach the crosswalk, I see a woman with a white cane. I slow down to ascertain what help she may or may not need. I remember my training program at the Helen Keller Institute. I refresh myself. Approach her gently. Do not presume that she wants or needs help. Let her express her wishes. Then, do not take her arm; if she wants assistance, she will take my arm. I am the one who knows where to walk, and she will follow my gentle lead, if she wants to. I pause. I breathe. I ask, "Would you like my assistance today?" "Sure," she says. "Sounds great." We walk companionably across the street. "Thank you," she says at the other side. "I know where I am now." I walk on ahead.

ૐ

As I approach the entrance to my synagogue, I see a young woman in a wheelchair approaching. Her musculature is not under ordinary control, but she is driving her chair very capably. Does she need my help? Why would she? She came here to go to temple on her own. There is a wheelchair access ramp around the back, but it's a long way to go. I hesitate and then approach her. "I don't mean to interfere with your progress, but if I can help you in any way, please let me know." She smiles up at me. "I can make it," she says. "See you inside. And thanks." It feels okay that I offered, and it's clear that she can manage, and likes to manage, herself.

❧

Many people with long-term illnesses want to give back to the world for all they have received. Even those who have asked for nothing and expected nothing unusual from their circle of friends find new ways to engage in the world that use their talents and their hearts. With illnesses that anticipate a return to normal health, there is the expectation that there will be opportunities to give to others. But with long-term illness, people may fear that they will always be on the receiving end and never in a position to give.

It is particularly important for those with chronic illness to offer themselves in whatever way they can, in order to preserve their wholeness. They speak of needing to decrease their sense of helplessness and normalize their place in the world. Often they can't give back directly to those who help them. Instead, they may find other avenues for being helpful.

Some people with physical limitations clip and send poems or cartoons to friends in need. Now, with the Internet, it is easy to send small gifts to people without leaving home. Some people give time to disease chat rooms on the Internet, or talk to people with a similar disease by phone; some work for hospice programs. Though it is hard for my friend George to leave his house, he talks his friends through their computer viruses, breakdowns, new software, and data loss by phone. He gets a great kick out of doing this for others.

❧

When Irene started to have back pain, she learned to rely on her coworkers to carry her papers from her desk to the main resource room. It was hard for her to get up and down all day while she bent over her microscope. The people in her department were delighted to help her in this way. It was no trouble for them, as they passed her desk, to pick up her out-box and move it for her. She had been a pleasant, reliable colleague for twenty years. But Irene needed to give back. When she went home in the evening and prepared a lovely dinner for her husband and two daughters, she found herself making extra for the people at work. She introduced them to homemade hummus and baba ghanoush long before they arrived on the supermarket shelves. Baklava and almond cookies from her fingers and into the office. Afterward, she began typing out the recipes for her coworkers, giving back to those who had helped her and allowing them, in turn, to give to others.

ॐ

With great pleasure, Meg, who walks with crutches, tells of counseling a young woman who was paralyzed at age twenty-nine. The woman spoke to Meg of wanting to die, and Meg surprised herself by saying, "That is always a choice."

Later, Meg saw the woman, in a wheelchair, with a baby on her lap. The woman told her that hearing the words, "That is always a choice," that day saved her life. Everyone else had been trying to talk her out of her feelings: "You'll feel differently soon. See how much you have to live for." By tuning in to the young woman's feelings with respect and acceptance, Meg gave her the freedom to find her own way up and out, and into life.

ॐ

Carol-Lynn had a neighbor, Lena, who had a difficult liver disease that hospitalized her for weeks when her child, Josh, was in preschool. Carol-Lynn did what she could to support the household while Lena was away. She checked in with Lena's husband and the child-care worker, and occasionally had Josh stay at her house for a few hours. Lena recovered. Years later, Carol-Lynn broke her leg and was on crutches for six weeks. Lena called Carol-Lynn and offered to have Josh walk Carol-Lynn's dog for her while she recovered. The mutual giving and receiving, the reciprocity of the arrangement, delighted Carol-Lynn.

è•

Late in the progression of Joseph's disease, he was no longer able to work, and he took up photography. He had never before had a creative form of expression; he thought that was for other people. Now, despite his growing weakness, he would go out into a nearby park early in the morning and take photos. Finding this means of self-expression kept him going longer than he expected. Toward the end of his life, he had a photography show, to which many people came, and he sold all of his photos. With great joy he donated all the funds to an organization that had helped him to find his way to photography when he needed it.

è•

Some people need to give directly to the giver, some give to others, and some engage in work to better the world. Giving time in whatever way they can, expressing their values and their gratitude through religious, political, and health organizations, people with chronic illness can find opportunities to give back.

There are no clear-cut words or actions that apply in every situation. These stories illustrate a range of reactions by people with chronic illness to the experience of giving and receiving. Together they demonstrate the importance of engaging in a conversation that allows us to hear what each person in the relationship wants and needs.

At any time, with no warning and no preparation, any one of us can have a calamity arrive at our door in the form of an armload of symptoms. It is not our fault. It's not in any of our life plans. All we can do is rise to the occasion and not fall prey to despair too often. Compassion for those who have been visited before you is the best gift you can give.

5. Patients Talk to Doctors; Doctors Talk to Patients

PATIENTS* TALK TO DOCTORS

During my in-hospital chemotherapy, my doctor came to see me every day. He had told me that he would be able to alleviate most of the side effects of treatment. He was reassuring, direct, and collegial. He would come into my large, airy room, lean against the desk with my family pictures behind him, and check in on how I was feeling, in detail. It was my job to make sure he heard me accurately as to every symptom, twitch, and question that I had. I had to learn to voice my concerns, not just say, "Everything is fine," as is my way. I had to plan which issues were important and needed to be stressed. He knew which questions to ask me, but there were conditions that arose for me that I needed to address with him.

❧

Sandy is very different from me. Where I use Canadian understatement, she uses Ethel Merman top decibels about all her symptoms. It was hard for her to contain herself, yet she knew she

* I have chosen to use the word "patient" in this chapter after omitting it from the rest of the book because it is linguistically parallel to "doctor."

needed to. She recognized that it was hard for her doctor to determine what needed attention and what was just her style. One day she tried lowering her voice and talking slowly. The whole exchange went better. She wished it were not her responsibility, when she was sick, to have to try on new ways of being, but given that it worked with her doctor, she acknowledged the usefulness of this new quieter style.

&

Before Glen would commit to treatment, he wanted to know exactly how he would feel each day and each week as he recovered. He was frightened, and as a planner by nature, it was hard for him not to know when he could go back to work, how long he would feel like working each day, how much energy he would have, and whether he had to wait two months to find out if the treatment had been successful. He kept asking and asking his doctor questions around these issues. Patiently the doctor reiterated how different the recovery is for each person. He told stories of the best- and worst-case scenarios. Finally, he addressed Glen's fears directly. "When we are fearful we try to get as many answers as possible as a way of alleviating the fear. But sometimes all we can do is say, 'I am afraid,' and try to live with that." Glen said that on hearing these words, he let go of the tension in his mind and body and was more able to allow the process to unfold.

Agnes was a reader. Textbooks, clinical trials, research reports, nothing was too much for her. She wanted to know what the odds of success were—for a person of her age and general health—of the various treatments she was reading about. She, like Glen, needed to know with a kind of desperation. She tried to compare the studies herself, but the studies were for small samples of people of unknown age and functioning level. Sometimes they reported response rate, sometimes the time until recurrence, and only occasionally were they able to measure the survival time, making it impossible for her to compare. She asked her doctor over and over, but there were no clear-cut answers. Her doctor was prescribing for her, given all that he knew, what he thought was her best option. He knew it was hard for her not to have clear measurable proof, but he did try to provide her with the justification that he was relying on. Gradually, as her trust in the doctor grew, as he spent time respectfully trying to answer her questions, Agnes was able to let go of needing all the answers.

❧

We do not have to accept the doctor that the hospital assigns to us. Clara interviewed eight doctors before she found the one she wanted to work with. She assessed whether each was willing to be aggressive in her treatment, and whether the doctor would find what seemed like the best form of treatment and use it—or use only treatments that were part of a proven protocol for a particular illness. Would they be willing to try an experimental treatment that might work but was not proved in her case? Would the doctor be willing to watch and wait if Clara felt that was called for? Clara compared her willingness to take risks to the doctor's risk level. She was interested in long-term survival over cure, and she tried to assess how comfortable each doctor felt with that outcome. The conversations allowed her to decide if this was a relationship that would become trusting and understanding, or not. Finally, Clara found a doctor she thought would suit her needs, even though it meant traveling some distance to see him.

ᐩ

Valerie went to a new doctor with all her records, slides, scans, and hopes. The doctor was trained in Western medicine and was also a Chinese medical practitioner. Valerie was hopeful. But toward the end of her visit, the doctor said to her, "This situation is very grave." Valerie went home from his office with more weight on her shoulders than when she entered. When she went back to the doctor to get the herbs he prescribed, she complained that he had not treated her in a way that worked for her; indeed, the prognosis might be grave, but could he not have added some words of comfort? The doctor apologized. And he restated his conclusion: "The situation is very grave, but you are a fighter, and we never really know what is going to happen, one person to the next." Valerie was pleased with herself, and she thanked the doctor for his apology.

ᐩ

Two months after her ovaries were removed because of a malignancy, Jordan returned to the hospital on an emergency basis. The pain from adhesions was enormous. She was hospitalized in preparation for a third surgery, running a fever and filled with dread of yet another round of pain and recovery. Her doctor, whom she was very fond of, ordered morphine for her. However, he neglected to tell her she might experience frightening nightmares as a side effect. That night Jordan began to hallucinate. Usually clearheaded, well-grounded, and rational, she was unaware that she was in an altered state. She believed that the chair in the corner was a demon that had come to hurt her. She pulled out her tubes and charged across the room to attack it. A natural athlete, Jordan has swum, surfed, sailed, and kayaked all her life. Even after all the cancer treatments, she was in better shape than most of us, and she made a lot of noise beating up the chair. A nurse heard her, came in the room, and talked Jordan back to reality. One of the things the nurse told her that night was that when a person has a high fever, it is well-known that morphine can produce the kind of experience Jordan had.

When she recovered, Jordan had a follow-up appointment with the doctor. She had always been comfortable with him, expressing her concerns easily, and she felt that he listened. But she had never before been critical of him or his plans for her. This time, not wanting to lose the ease between them—and not wanting to pretend she was not angry with him—she needed to find a way to talk to him without deserting her true feelings and without pushing him away. She thought long and hard how to present her issue. During the appointment she surprised herself by starting to cry, and she spoke about how hurt, rather than how angry, she was. And her doctor listened. He sat with her; he told her he had not known this had happened to her, and he was glad she could tell him. She was relieved. She also recognized that in putting forth her vulnerable, hurt feelings rather than a hard, angry attack, she got her doctor's attention.

Once she and her doctor had talked, Jordan felt that in spite of her doctor's mistake, she *did* want to go on working with him. She was proud of her success at reaching her doctor, and she hoped he had learned something from her.

≈

When John was told that he had only a limited time to live, no matter what medical treatments were used, he decided he did not want an aggressive, debilitating treatment, even though it might give him a little more time. Instead he opted for a light protocol that would keep him comfortable and aware for what might be a shorter amount of time.

The doctor used his knowledge base to determine the best course of action for John. He described with care the long- and short-term consequences of decisions. John could stay in the hospital and receive intravenous medications that would limit his mobility, or he could go home, receive hospice care for pain relief, and die comfortably in familiar surroundings.

John and his doctor arrived at this second option together by careful listening and planning. This kind of a conversation between patient and doctor is an essential part of healing. To participate in the decision, John drew upon his strength and commitment, improving the chance that the treatment would make a difference.

୨ଧ

Some people, on the other hand, like to be told what to do and do not want a collaborative process. They trust that the doctor knows what is best for them, and they rely on that. Doing their own research and participating in any choices that may occur is not what they want. There are doctors out there who are willing to direct such patients and take full responsibility for the decisions.

୨ଧ

In a state of extreme sensitivity brought on by her illness, Trish realized that her doctor, Fred, more than anyone else, could alarm and unnerve her. Intellectually, she knew that he was only a person, but as she entered the world of cancer, she found that she was very poor at keeping her reactivity under control. He was the one who read her scans and tests and told her what they meant. And the results of the scans dictated whether or not she needed treatment and thus her emotional state for the next few months of her life.

She tried to talk herself into maintaining her own inner calm, hearing the doctor's information as just facts and not exaggerating the importance of everything he said in her fear. This was hard for her. But once she realized this about herself, she worked on not getting caught in her pattern of thinking. Gradually her relationship with her doctor normalized, and she was no longer tempted to hang on his every word.

Marcia realized that her doctor was as emotionally unavailable when giving good news as when giving bad news. Once, he told her that her bone marrow test had been clear of cancer in the same flat way that he talked about treatments for osteoporosis. Her husband had to ask, "This is good news, is it not?" "Yes," the doctor said, "this is good news."

Marcia had five years to get to know her doctor. Finally she said, "When I leave here I feel worse than any other time in this cancer journey. I need you to ask me, 'How are you doing with this news?' so I can release my feelings of dread or sadness or concern before I leave here." She felt much better after she told her doctor this. Even after that, he often failed to ask her about her feelings; but she had stated her case and taken care of herself in an important way. Somehow, by stating her needs, Marcia found that they diminished.

Norma often had to sit for four hours in the waiting room before meeting with her doctor to find out if there had been tumor growth or not. Dreading these waits, she began to get tense approximately forty-eight hours before tests and appointments. She would walk around for two days telling herself how well she was doing this time. But then she'd have to wait for four hours, which depleted all her reserves. Norma never told her doctor this; if she had, he might have been able to schedule her appointment at a time when she would not have to wait for so long.

Ellie, too, felt extremely tense as she entered her doctor's office. She wanted him to respond to her emotional needs as well as her physical changes. Those desires were never met. Though she realized that her doctor was not capable of responding to her in a supportive way, she decided not to leave him. She had faith in his clinical ability, and for her this was more important than anything else. On her own, Ellie found places of comfort outside the doctor's office. Her friends, her family, her acupuncturist, her yoga teacher, and her support group filled the gap.

DOCTORS TALK TO PATIENTS

Sometimes a doctor and patient don't work well together. And even if they do, a patient may want another opinion. It is always legitimate for a patient to seek out another opinion. Doctors are used to this. Sometimes the doctor initiates the referral. One doctor cautions his patients to be sure to choose a doctor who knows more than he does. He often suggests a referral and will consult with the other doctor. Never fear that by asking for another opinion you will offend your doctor. And if you do offend the doctor, you might want to question what's going on with the doctor and whether he or she is the right person for you.

❧

To get the best medical care, learn the name of a staff person in the doctor's office who seems helpful, or to whom you connect easily. Ask for these people by name when you call with questions. They can often answer. Build a relationship with them as well as with the doctor.

If you want questions answered, you may be able to send a fax or e-mail with a phone number and ask your questions, briefly, in writing. Or send a brief fax or e-mail before a visit. The doctor will be more prepared to answer you. One of the doctors I spoke to suggests to patients that they tape-record their sessions with him. Then they can refer back to the actual conversation, and there will be no doubt about what the doctor said. There is no need to be embarrassed by coming in to an appointment ready to tape. Another doctor I know records the session herself and gives the patient the tape at the end of their visit together.

❧

Doctors expect patients to bring someone with them; it's not a breach of etiquette. I take my husband with me to all appointments so he can make notes and so we can discuss everything later. The discrepancies between what each of us thinks we heard only underscore the importance of another pair of ears in these emotionally charged encounters. On one occasion, when my doctor put my X-rays up on a screen, I saw how large some of the lymph nodes had become, and that was the last thing I saw or heard for about thirty minutes. The rest was a complete blank. The fact that the doctor said the nodes were still not large enough to treat, that they were not resting on any organs or closing off any arteries was immaterial; I couldn't take anything in. Later, over lunch, Charlie was able to tell me all these reassuring facts, which I had been unable to hear.

My friend Tanya wanted a baby. She married in her late thirties, and she and her husband cherished the dream of having a family. But she did not conceive. Tanya and her husband consulted many doctors, both conventional and unconventional. They went through many appointments, treatments, and diagnostic workups. And each doctor repeated that, given Tanya's physiology, conceiving and bearing a child was not going to happen. This was hard to accept. Tanya decided to consult one more highly regarded and highly expensive expert. With hope in her heart, Tanya went to this last appointment, was poked and prodded one more time, and then received this blunt message on her answering machine: "It's true, you are barren." Tanya still feels the pain of that moment ten years later.

❧

It was the job of the oncology nurse to describe the side effects of chemotherapy I was about to receive. She took me into a small, poorly lit office, and for half an hour she outlined what could happen to my body from the four chemicals I was going to take. She had a soft, flat voice. "Your gums may bleed; you may be nauseous; your hair will fall out, public and pubic; your eyebrows and lashes will go last; food will taste strange; liquor will taste worse; your nails will weaken; your heart may be damaged; you may have constipation or diarrhea; you may be greatly fatigued" . . . and on and on. She listed the various pills and mouthwashes I could take to reduce some of these conditions. At the very end, in a mechanical way, she said, "Probably nothing bad will happen, and it may not be as bad as I described, but this is my job." And she left the room. I hardly heard her last statement and because it was put out in such a pro forma way, I didn't believe it. In the end she was right, nothing bad happened, but the fear and dread induced by her recital of side effects was at the time overwhelming.

❧

A friend of mine was called back for repeated scans for his stomach distress. No possibilities of what the condition was were offered to him. After two and a half weeks had passed, he was called into the radiologist's office and told, "Well, it's malignant." Just that. No preparation, no sympathy, no explanation.

It's important to remember that statistics are just numbers. They are not about individuals; they reflect a range of possibilities. Presented bluntly, these generalizations can be deeply disturbing to patients. Many people have arrived at my group shaken by being told, "Why would you do that complicated surgery? You're going to die in eighteen months anyway." "If you don't take my advice, you will die in two months." "You are going to live for two years." "The situation is very serious." "There is nothing we can do." "There is no proof that anything works." These strong statements coming from a doctor often undermine the hope of the patient.

James's mother died suddenly, and only weeks later, his sick father had to be taken to the intensive care unit. All night James stayed with his father, taking care of those little needs that don't require a nurse—going out to the hall for help when it was needed, holding his father's hand, and trying hard to do what he could to ease his father's discomforts. In the morning, his father's doctor came by, looked at the chart, and barked into the room, "Don't try to micromanage this, James." Then he walked away.

A doctor who is a friend of mine told me about James. My friend is usually mild-mannered, but his reaction to this story was strong; he was really angry about the doctor who had attacked James. He kept saying over and over again, "I would have fired that doctor if I had been him. No way I would have kept that doctor."

&

Medical education now includes training in how to deal compassionately with patients. One doctor friend told me about what she would include in a training program for doctors. She would arrange for a weekend or longer during which doctors could explore their reactions to their own experiences with pain, illness, and receiving help. She would have doctors ask themselves these questions, and spend time visualizing or putting words to the answers:

Think about a time when you were hurting.
What was helpful at those times?
Who was helpful, and how did the person do that?
What did you not like?
How was it to receive?
What was healing?
How did the person offer healing?
Was the setting comforting to you?
Picture yourself offering those qualities that you found
    helpful to your patients.

᠊ᕀ

Think about a time when you helped a friend or loved one.
How do you feel and behave differently with a patient?
What might you do differently?
Allow yourself time to remember your feelings when a
    patient died. How did you express your feelings?
To whom?
How do you block your feelings?
What does that do to your body?
What does that do to your personal relationships?

What does that do to the relationship with the significant
  others of your patient?
What have you learned from this?
What might you do differently next time?

&

Alex felt very sick. He went to his internist first. The internist
performed some tests and told Alex he could have any of several
problems—one being a faulty heart valve, but not to get fixated on
that until he had seen the cardiologist. Alex tried to stay neutral
about the possibilities until all the facts were in. The cardiologist
did some tests and, at the same time, set up a date for a return
appointment. That way, whatever the news, Alex would not
receive a call asking him to make an appointment, striking fear
into his heart. Nor would the doctor have to tell Alex the news on
an answering machine.

Alex's doctor had followed a systematic plan for allowing the
news to be given, whatever it was, as well as possible. The internist
laid the groundwork, so there were no complete surprises, and the
cardiologist followed through with similar sensitivity. By the time
Alex appeared for his follow-up appointment with the cardiologist, he was emotionally as prepared as he could be for the news.
And indeed it was bad news. "I am so sorry to tell you this," the
doctor said. "There is no good way to tell you this, and I wish you
didn't have this in your life, but I'm here to help you through the

necessary treatments. Together, with your strength of character and my expertise, we can deal with whatever comes."

৵

After chemotherapy had ended I found during the second week at home that I was more nauseous and fatigued than I expected—and I was tired of it. My doctor listened with care and suggested that I drop one of the pills I was taking. It could be the culprit. I did. The next morning I woke up feeling strong and able. I was able to be clear about my symptoms, and my doctor was able to listen fully.

Ralph, a doctor, encourages listening long and carefully to patients. This is the best way not only to understand what they're feeling but also to learn how to tell them bad news or even to make a plan for care with them. In giving them information, he feels, it is important to tell the truth but to couch it in hope.

I am here to give you the best care I can.
This is a difficult disease to cure, but you may live for some
    time with it.
This is hard to cure, but some people do recover.
There is a chance that X will make a difference.
Whenever it should happen that you die, if I am still your
    doctor, I will do all I can to help you have a peaceful death.

Using language that patients understand is important. Saying, "You have an inoperable brain tumor," sounds to many patients like a death sentence. In fact, "inoperable" means simply that the tumor cannot be removed surgically. There may well be treatments that will reduce the tumor, prolong life, and even make the tumor disappear. If "inoperable" is not defined, the patient might well go away in despair.

Doctors can say things to call forth the natural instinct of the body to heal and the natural desire of the mind to hope while still presenting the limits imposed by reality.

> The prognosis for your illness is not good, but there are people who have defied the odds.
> There are stories of miraculous recoveries.
> We will do all we can to help you with your condition, and you never know what might work.
> It's not your fault if it doesn't work, but we will work together to keep you as well as possible for as long as possible.

When my doctor had to tell me that my lymphoma was changing from a nonthreatening, slow-growing disease to a mix of cells that included some faster-growing lymphoma, he sat down near me and looked into my eyes. He leaned toward me, kind and sympathetic. "We will have to treat this more aggressively, you know," he said softly. "I will help you make the necessary decisions. I know that you and your husband like to consult with other doctors, and that will be fine. Don't take too long. I am here to help you synthesize all you learn. We are a team."

I liked it when my doctor told me, "I will help you get through this." He even said, "We will get through this together." The fact that I remember these simple statements is proof of the power of his words. For a doctor to say to a person, "I will be with you," is a simple statement—brief and heartfelt. The patient knows how hard those statements are to make, especially for a physician as opposed to a loved one, and appreciates both the effort and the message.

It is also very warming to be told, "I know that you will get through this with style/courage/strength/humor/valor." I have found simple statements like this encouraging. Doctors do not usually talk to patients about their strengths, so if a doctor were to comment that I am a healthy, capable person, it would be affirming and supportive, and add to the strength already in me. Imagine if a doctor said, "Given the number of people I treat, I see you have [name a special capacity] and that will help carry the day for you." We all have qualities that will get us through some or all of what lies ahead, and to have a doctor remind us of these attributes gives a great deal of support.

➴

When Gene entered medical school he wanted to care for people and serve them, particularly in matters relating to their bodies. But he quickly learned that the mind, heart, and body are one, and that they all need attention. The best way to connect with other people is by truly listening to them. Without a point to make, without a goal to reach, just listening allows more information to come than when the information is shaped by a question. Of course, it is unrealistic in today's world to think that an hour of listening to a patient is in the realm of possibility for most doctors. However, Gene discovered that if he spoke a little less and listened a little more to the patient as a whole person, not just a collection of symptoms, he learned a great deal in the allotted time. He liked to ask his patients what gave meaning to their life, when they have felt most successful, how they would like to be remembered. Knowing these things helped Gene to personalize health care to each person.

Emma, a patient of Gene's in her eighties, had uterine cancer, which became painful when she walked. She told him she did not want surgery, but she wanted to be able to go back to her modern dance class. Gene listened closely to her concerns and told her what her options were and what surgery could offer her. In the end she chose to have the surgery and was able to dance for two more years.

❧

When Lucy was choosing oncologists, Joy went to meet the doctors with her. This is a stressful time, as the treatment plans, the feel of the hospital, and the personality of the doctor can all differ radically, and a big decision hangs in the balance. Having a backup person to confer with afterward was a great benefit to Lucy. It also put the doctor on notice in an interesting way. Joy is more inquisitive than Lucy, and she asked a lot of questions. At one point Lucy asked a doctor for another CAT scan before treatment began. The doctor responded that he would order an additional CAT scan for Lucy—rather than having to answer to Joy.

Geoffrey, another doctor I know, realized early in his work that he needed to deal with the family members of patients as well as the patients themselves. He needed to elicit their support, answer their questions, relieve their anxiety, and keep them informed. Time, attention, kindness, and awareness were important in these exchanges as well, and sometimes these were in short supply. What Geoffrey has learned to do, he told me, is find the leader in the family power structure and connect with that person, who then passes the information on to other family members.

❧

When Maude, a nurse's aide from New York Hospital, had a heart attack, the ambulance that picked her up was directed to take her to Saint Luke's Hospital, since that was closest to the scene of the incident. A doctor in the ambulance, taking the time to listen to Maude, learned that she worked at New York Hospital. And he realized that being with her colleagues, at a hospital she knew, would aid in her recovery. The doctor checked with Maude to see if her own hospital would suit her better. She immediately responded yes. So he made ar-

rangements from the ambulance to have her taken across town
to New York Hospital.

∂⋅

After chemotherapy, when I was complaining that my energy had
not returned after five weeks, my doctor commented, ever so
politely, that from what he knew of me, I was expecting to do too
much. His words made me smile. I felt he had seen me as a whole
person. His comment did help me keep my expectations at a more
reasonable level.

Both doctors and patients need to be comfortable in the doctor-
patient relationship, and can appreciate it. One doctor friend said
to me that what gives him joy is working with each person, seeing
him or her change, and building a relationship over a long period
of time. He likes to get calls from his patients between visits when
they need him. He enjoys talking to them and is happy to supply
them with any information they need.

∂⋅

Barbara is a doctor in a large public hospital in Washington, D.C.
She deals with people from every country in the world and has
discovered the value of connecting with important family members as a way of learning the family's particular culture and
expectations around health and illness. Knowing more about
the customs helps her plan her interventions. She has learned
to ask how a particular family deals with death and the dying

process. Who is allowed to visit? How do they talk about dying and with whom? How are the funeral and mourning carried out? Then she modulates her interventions to meet their needs.

る

While doctors are trained to cure more than to help with dying, and while their major activities are focused on continuing life, there comes a point where the organism turns to death. Doctors can play an important role in reducing suffering for the bereaved in those moments. However, many doctors are afraid to confront death. They call the nurse and leave the scene. One young woman said that after talking with the doctor daily for many weeks at the end of her husband's life, she was surprised that after his death it took the doctor three weeks to call. He had helped her make so many important decisions, including when it was time to remove her young husband's life support system. The doctor meant so much to her during those last weeks. Yet what about her life-support system? Where was he at the end? Wasn't he mourning too?

る

When Tina was diagnosed with a recurrence, she went to her doctor and asked him if he was prepared to see her through the end-of-life process. Tina wanted to have a doctor who did not turn dying patients over to nurses and family. She wanted to have an experienced and calm doctor with her in death. Not only did he assure her that he would not abandon her at the end, he also told her that he understood as an oncologist that dying was an important part of his work. However, he told her, if she was asking about "physician-assisted suicide," he was not willing to help her with that. Tina left his office reassured that she was in the hands of a doctor who had thought through the end-of-life issues she was concerned about.

৵

A group of doctors I heard about designed an exercise to practice saying good-bye to patients and, ultimately, to their own loved ones. At their last team meeting each spring, they spoke words of appreciation to each other. Not words of correction, or even hopes for their future, just appreciation for who each person was and what he or she meant to the speaker. They went around the whole group, giving each member a chance to say a few words to each other member. This is not easy to do, and in recognizing the difficulty they came to appreciate the value of this kind of acknowledgement with others and for others. They realized that in this way, they might offer their words of love to a person who is dying.

৵

One doctor I know, Warren, has sometimes played a role in the mourning process with his patients. After one patient named David died, the family spent many hours in the hospital with David's body, distressed and crying and comforting each other.

Warren stayed with them. The kind of intimacy that arises in these personal moments is what gives meaning to his work. Several of the patient's family members asked him if they could see him later. He recognized that they needed to talk about the death, to understand it better, to find some place of peace with the loss.

Warren sat with them that evening and gently tried to explore their feelings. Mourning can often be prolonged and complicated by feelings that family members or the doctor did something wrong, that if they had acted differently, their loved one would be alive. With David's family, the doctor had an opportunity to alleviate those feelings. He sat with them and asked each person in turn, "What would you have done differently, or do you wish had been done differently, when David was dying?" As they gave their answers, Warren explained, without being defensive, how the result would have been the same, even if that other route had been taken. It was David's time to die. Warren told them about the services in the community for the bereaved. Then he called the family a week later to check in. He was moved by the words of David's widow, who thanked him for his time that night and said how much it had meant to all of them to understand fully how the decisions were made. She felt so much better for having had the conversation.

⁊❧

Another doctor, Richard, tells me that he does not like to cry with patients. He feels that it's his job to be in control of his emotions enough to comfort the bereaved. But he told me this story from early in his medical practice. One evening, Karen, a patient he had cared for over the last six months, died. He had become attached to this patient. He had even come in to see her on his day off, so strong had the relationship grown. Her aunt, who raised her, was with Karen that evening. Richard sat by the bed watching Karen breathe her last breaths. He breathed with her, and when the breathing stopped, he found himself in tears, sitting at her side. He was reminded of the death of his brother when he was a teenager, and he felt he was shedding the tears that he hadn't on that occasion. He didn't want to turn to the aunt for comfort; he had no experience with this overflow of feeling, being young and new to his practice. He left the room briefly, cried in the hall, and then returned to be with Karen's aunt. Now, many years later, he feels he did the right thing in the situation. The aunt felt so cared for by Richard that she became his patient. He is now more aware of when his own feelings might come up and has learned ways of supporting himself while caring for others, without backing away from the painful moments.

❧

Jeanne, who was hospitalized, asked people to pray with her. Peter, her doctor, a man of science and not of the church, was invited to pray too. He had never prayed before. And yet he found himself at his patient's bedside, holding her hand, with words in his mouth he had never said before: "God, please guide and protect your servant, Jeanne, in her journey to your side. May she find comfort there, and know that here on earth she is missed and mourned." Peter surprised himself, but he realized how much this meant to Jeanne and how much it helped him see her through the end of her life.

ð

Rather than divorcing himself from the end stage, another doctor I spoke to, Doug, found that if he was present at the death of a patient, he carried the memory of that patient with less pain. Partly it was seeing the body with no life force and partly it was the comfort from being with others who were present and feeling the loss together.

ð

In the past, some doctors, and especially interns and residents who are still new to the field, have experienced depression from repeated losses. Now there is an effort to help people achieve some acceptance by acknowledging the sadness of each loss. One young man told me he likes to wish the spirit of the deceased well before going back to work. Talking about the intensity of the experience with the other staff members helps other doctors feel the feelings and yet step beyond them into awareness of the loss, grief, helplessness, sadness, and then acceptance of the feelings.

ð

One young doctor, Calle, realized that the meditation practice she had developed during her pregnancy in preparation for childbirth was serving her well in her relationship to dying patients. By centering herself in her place of internal calm, she could attend to the patient much more easily. When she was in the presence of suffering in the hospital, with just a few focused breaths she could bring herself into the place of calm attention. Other doctors noted that she appeared to have a way to calm herself and asked about it. She began teaching a simple breath meditation to her colleagues.

Sitting quietly in a chair, legs uncrossed, hands in her lap, eyes closed, Calle taught the doctors to bring their attention to the in breath and the out breath—to feel the air pass into their nostrils and out of their nostrils—and to sit, focusing on their breath, for twenty minutes a day. When their mind wanders, she suggested that they bring it gently back to the breath. It is natural for the mind to wander. The practice is to bring the awareness back to the breath, sooner and sooner, without judgment. Practicing this simple breathing meditation allowed her, during her busy day, to return to that place of quiet, nonjudgmental awareness from which she could focus on the task at hand.

❧

These stories include a number of experiences from people who have had good relationships with their doctors, and from doctors who care deeply about their patients and try to serve them beyond just their physical care. Too often, people talk only about the terrible experiences they have had with the medical profession. And there are many such stories. But there is also a possibility of something better: the possibility of entering a relationship with a doctor and expecting a healing encounter—and when the pump needs priming, or some fine-tuning needs to be done, patients not shying away from the kind of engagement they want. Doctors too can help to fine-tune their interactions with patients, so that the relationship works for both parties with respect and appreciation.

6. At the End of Life

The Earth and the Sky live forever
  The reason the Earth and the Sky live forever
  Is that they do not live only for themselves, alone
And therefore, they live on in everything.

—Lao Tzu

We all will die. This we know. What we do not know is when or how. Many people die suddenly and unexpectedly. Some people die more slowly, with time for conversations about how and where they might want to die, expressions of love, reminiscences, and farewells. Some of us may get to say whom we want to attend to us at the end, what we are feeling about the process; we may have a chance to offer forgiveness and ask for it from those we have hurt. There are possibilities for improving relationships even at the end of life. Words of love and sorrow and reconciliation often come out as death approaches. Both the person who is dying and those in attendance may find that there is a refinement of each moment. Only the essentials matter. Feelings that are not spoken on ordinary days may be expressed at the end of a life.

But death is not always as tidy as this implies. It may be

unexpected. Sometimes a person dies in the middle of a game of tennis, or crossing the street, or in a war. There may be no time or ability to plan ahead, to say good-bye—and that is something that the mourners have to live with. Or one member of the family in the circle of care may be unable to do anything but cry, or drink, or be angry. Then it is hard to pursue a calm, reasonable plan and gentle expressions of feeling.

This chapter is designed for people who have the opportunity and want to examine their lives as they die, who want to explore the experience and share it with those around them. It is for people who are hoping to care for friends and relatives during the process of dying and want to do it well. Mostly, it is for people who want to face death, plan for it, to whatever extent is possible, say some good-byes, and surrender to the unknown when the time comes.

Pain medication can ease the end of life, making it possible to be conscious and communicative. It can also make us less conscious. Illness and the body's response to it can nullify some of our plans and wishes. Even the best planning can't take into account every eventuality. There needs to be room for the unpredictable nature of death. Sometimes miracles can happen and delay the whole process far past the expected final moment. Other times, death arrives more quickly than we expect.

By offering a variety of experiences of people who are dying and those who attend to them, I hope to enlarge the range of perspectives on death, the reactions to it, and the plans we make. By representing others' experiences at the end of life, I hope to show caregivers how to hear expressions of fear, anger, sadness, and joy in an accepting, nonjudgmental way. I hope that people who are dying will be able to formulate more easily what they want to say and do about their death.

I offer words of comfort for caregivers and people at the end their life. I review some acts of kindness for the bedside of the dying person. I explore ways of listening and responding to mourners. These ideas are not so different from those I discussed in the previous chapters about dealing with people who are ill. But with death itself approaching, the situation is more intense—and more one-directional.

All aspects of dying bear discussion—the medical, legal, emotional, spiritual, and intellectual. It is important to allow the person facing imminent death to do as much of the planning and deciding as possible. If he or she is not able to do so, it then falls to those who are in attendance. The more conversation that has preceded the final stage, the easier it is for those offering care.

I have described some "good deaths," so that ideas for yourself and others may emerge and become more likely to be fulfilled. A "good death" includes time for good-byes, for loose ends to be closed, for loved ones to gather, for a degree of consciousness, close to the end, and a sense of completion, resolution, and acceptance in both the person who is dying and the loved ones.

After death there are many different forms of mourning. Again, I recount some of these as a way to be accepting of what occurs in your family or with your loved ones. The forms that grief takes are as many as there are people, and we need to accept each other's way of letting go.

Death is a subject that most of us can entertain for only a few minutes at a time, if at all. To dare to do so for long—to touch the feelings, to look at the options, the opportunity it gives us—is to fully engage in the potential for consciousness that we possess as humans.

ॐ

Three women: an older woman, a younger woman, and I, all diagnosed with lymphoma, are lying back in turquoise plastic-covered recliners in a chemotherapy infusion room. Three women, three computer-controlled infusion trees, three technicians fulfilling their roles for three hours. Liquids dripping. The younger woman, age forty, with two small children at home, says, "I'm gonna die, I know it, I'm gonna die. Cancer means you're going to die. Whatever will I do? Why sit here? I'm gonna die."

I, age fifty-nine, grandparent of three, and a walking optimist, say, "Cancer does not mean you're going to die. Lots of people get better. My mother had a mastectomy at forty-nine and lived to ninety, when she died of something else. I'm not planning to die anytime soon. I have to see my grandchildren grow up. There are many kinds of lymphoma that don't kill people."

The third woman, age seventy-five, says, "I'm a great-grand-mother, and I say, 'What's so bad about dying?'"

Three different perspectives from three different places in the life cycle. The oldest woman has had more time to face the fact that she will die one day and is therefore more resigned to it. She has lived her life, has few regrets, she tells us, and she does not want a long period of pain and suffering. The alternative, death, looks okay to her.

The young woman, with two young children, is filled with fear. She is in a life phase that requires her to keep on living. To leave her children without a mother is untenable to her. She cannot give credence to the other positions that are stated that day. Choked as she is by her fear, she insists that cancer is a death sentence.

My own half denial that I will die is another kind of narrow vision. I might, after all, die from this disease. Medical science does not know how to save many people. My body's own immune system is not working. I can carry in my consciousness for moments at a time the idea that I can die, but I push it away. It's not the outcome I would choose.

There are other positions along this continuum, from clinging to life to giving in to death. All of us, in the midst of a life-threatening illness, find ourselves at different places on the continuum on different days, at different moments. What I value is the ability to watch my feelings flow along the spectrum, to watch them change, and to know they will change again.

ᘑ

I went to see my friend Winfield and his lover, Russell, when they were both fading from AIDS. What was I to say to them? I wanted

to know what it is like to face dying, and I knew that Win would
be willing to talk about it. I created scenarios in my head of what I
would ask. But I did not want to express my fears; I did not want to
put negative thoughts in their minds; I did not want to burden
them or make them feel I was rushing them out of life. In the end,
I froze up in their presence. I never said how much Win meant to
me, how helpful he had been to my marriage, my children, and me.
I never said how I admired his calm, thoughtful, loving way, how
much his comments, without judgment, had helped me in moments of indecision, or how empowered I felt when I talked with
him at other moments.

The last time I saw Win alive, I chattered away our time
together. And then he died. I regret that I did not dare to speak
the questions I carried. I wanted to know what it was like for him
to look death in the face, to know that his time on earth was
limited. I wanted to know how it felt each day, as he grew weaker.
I wanted him to teach me about dying. And he would have. He
had talked with other friends about his curiosity about death and
his desire to die as consciously as possible. I regret that I did not
tell him how much he meant to me, but I did give him a large long
hug at the end, and perhaps, just maybe, that said enough.

I have since learned that I need to determine, from my knowledge of my friends, whether I will frighten them by talking about
the possibility of death. In most cases they have already had many
thoughts on the subject. But I do tread with great care in this area.
I have learned this from my own experience with lymphoma.

When I have thought I was facing death, there were very few people to whom I would have talked about my thoughts on dying. But a simple question—"Do you ever think this illness could end in death?"—would have allowed me to answer simply no or, expanding on the question, to tell someone all my thoughts about death from the moment of diagnosis. I made different choices about what to discuss at different moments. Sometimes I revealed the irrational fears that went through my head in the middle of the night, or talked about what I had been reading, or told how I tried to address the real possibility that I might die much sooner than I had expected. I learned how not to talk when I did not want to, and I discovered what to say to different people about the possibility of my dying.

༈

In 1963, my uncle Sol, a judge on the Court of Appeals of Pennsylvania, was dying of colon cancer. A calm, educated man, he was deprived by his doctors of the information that he was dying. They thought they were doing the right thing. At the return of the cancer the doctors told only his business partner. Later, they told his wife, who told her children. But Sol himself was never told that he would soon die. Presumably he knew he was dying. That he was staying in bed at home all day with his son and wife in attendance must have suggested that all was not well, but no one talked to him about his death, nor did he talk about it. The care given to him, he surely knew, was an act of love. His silence too was perceived as an act of love in that era.

The approach to death and dying has changed in the last forty years in America. People are usually told about their situation. Books and articles are available to people who are ill, full of statistics, treatment choices, tales of spontaneous remissions, and information on alternative healers. There is a culture of revelation and conversation. Choices and decisions rely largely on the wishes of the person dying, though in some subcultures, and with people who have expressly said they do not want to know their prognosis, there is still the option of not telling, not talking.

Through my work with people who are facing their death, I have found that most people want to have a conversation about their feelings, at some point. There are refinements around when and with whom this conversation may take place. Some people prefer to talk to a nurse, a doctor, or a therapist. Some talk easily to a spouse; some prefer a relative who is less immediately affected by the impending death. Some have a close friend they trust with their thoughts and feelings.

When those who face death begin such conversations, they can leave the listener stumbling for ways to respond.

ھ

I was sitting in a hospital room with a friend who is in her eighties and failing in health. I asked her what she called that quality in herself that keeps on keeping on. She said she did not know what to call it, but that sometimes she thought, "Enough already." This felt like a big opening to me, but I was very hesitant about how to step into it. Here I was, just another woman, a person for whom she did not need to stay alive. I was open to having a conversation about living and dying, but in my momentary pause, gathering my thoughts about how to keep the conversation going and what to say next, she was on to another subject, and the door closed. Maybe what she told me was all she wanted to say. I will never know.

What if I had asked her

Are you serious about not wanting to keep on going?
Is that a thought you have often?
How will you know when is enough?
What makes you want to keep on going?
What deaths have you experienced?
Have you pictured your death? What would it be like?

&

I have a friend from childhood whose husband had a difficult heart problem and was in and out of the hospital for years. He would jokingly say that he was going to live forever. And he never talked seriously about the possibility of death. Dahlia needed to know about his insurance and his wishes for care at death and the funeral, but she didn't know how to talk to him. "He never raises the subject," she told me one day. I asked her what kept her from raising the subject. She looked surprised by the question but then realized that she could indeed say, "I need to know what you want." I suggested to her that she talk to him about her feelings before she asked him about the practical issues. She wanted to talk about her love for him, about her pride in their sons, about her fears of being alone, about missing him, about wanting to die too. Dahlia hoped he would say words of love and comfort to her in return.

Dahlia was also concerned about the business side of death. Some of the questions on her mind were

Do you want to be buried or cremated? And where?

Do you want a service? If so, where? Do you have wishes for your service?

Are there people you want me to call when you die?

Can you tell me about your investments, lawyers, and insurance?

Is there money in banks or investments that I don't know about?

When she had raised these issues in the past, her husband shut down, changed the subject, or disappeared into the bathroom with a book. Now Dahlia primed herself to gently remind him that she would raise this subject again—and that she needed answers. One night, as Dahlia began talking to Leo, he picked up a newspaper and went to the bathroom, as usual. But this time, she followed him, stood outside the door, and teased him, saying that she had known he would do this, and she was not quitting. She needed to talk. And they did.

Much of what Dahlia needed to hear was covered that first night, and then a few weeks later, she opened the subject again. There was more on her mind. Leo had been very reluctant to discuss this matter, because his finances, taxes, and debts were not in order—and that was painful to him. However, Dahlia needed to know, and somewhere in himself, he knew he would have to reveal the information before he died. Once they talked, they began to work together to clear up the financial problems. With the practical issues dealt with, they were more able to concentrate on their relationship and their good-byes. In the end, Leo was pleased that Dahlia had done this for them.

❧

Many of us would like to be the one to receive the wisdom and the fears of the person who is dying. Others of us are unable to bear that conversation. It is important to assess which role you want to play. Is there someone closer who can be open to the emotions as they arise? Is it your need to have this conversation, or is it the dying person's? We may need to ask, "Do you have someone to talk to about dying? Would you like me to be with you as you put words around your experience?" And we need to be willing to accept that it might not be our place.

I have heard of people who have died without finding the right time or person to whom to reveal themselves. Then the closest survivor does not know what arrangements have been made for the person who has died, and there have been no good-byes. In this case, the needs of the closest survivor may have to take precedence over the needs of the person who is dying. The survivor's need to have a conversation may outweigh the reluctance of the dying person.

I have found that an easy entry into the subject is to begin by comparing beliefs about death, dying, and the afterlife. With people who are scientific in their approach to life, who are older than I am, or whom I don't know that well, I would use the following approach. The responses are usually calm and curious, and the discussion paves the way to speaking out loud the fears, plans, wishes, and feelings about the dying process and death.

Conversations about beliefs could include

What do you think happens when the body dies?

Do you believe in a soul?

Do you believe in an afterlife?

What will the afterlife look like?

Do you believe in hell?

Do you believe in God?

Do you believe you can make any difference in what happens in the hereafter?

When and how would you like to die?

Conversation starters with people with whom I am intimate, or who are younger than I am, might include the following questions:

> When you were seven, what did you think happened at death?
> Who was the first person you knew who died?
> What did you think happened to him or her?
> What did your family teach you about an emotional response to death?
> How has your thinking changed?
> What do you believe now?
> What do you think it will be like—the after-death experience?
> Have you ever been with someone as he or she died? What was that like for you?
> What are your fears about dying and being dead?
> What do you believe about reincarnation?

Death has become so much the province of professionals that some of us have no experience and tremendous fear. Bringing those fears into the room is not helpful to the person who is dying. Caregivers who have had experience with death bring greater ease to the task than newcomers. But sometimes there are no old hands around. Informing ourselves through books and self-examination can also bring us to a place of enough ease to attend a loved one's death with an open mind and an open heart.

❧

When Annabel's ex-husband was dying, she went to visit him. Though both had remarried ten years before, she found she needed to go back and see him again. The visits grew in number. She asked him at one point, "How is it that I am the one who has become your primary caregiver?" He said to her, "You are not afraid of dying, and you can use the word 'death.'"

Annabel had experienced the loss of a brother when she was young and had nursed both her parents in their final years. By the time she sat down with her ex-husband, she was not afraid of death. He knew this about her. Not all caregivers have had the experience that Annabel brought to the bedside, but finding our way to accept the inevitability of death will make us better able to help.

❧

When I think a person does not know how to begin talking, but wants to, I have asked

Do you find your mind producing a lot of fears at three A.M.?
    What comes up for you then?
What are your thoughts about dying?
What do you fear about dying?

What do you consider a "good" death?

If you could die anywhere, where would you like to be?

A mountain, a seashore, a special room somewhere?

Whom do you want with you as you are dying?

ও

Before caregivers ask these questions, they need to know what their own answers are. In order to listen well, and then discuss with someone else what dying means to them, we need to be familiar with our own hopes, fears, and wishes. Caregivers might center themselves for such a conversation by reviewing in their mind some of their irrational thoughts and some of the ways they feel they have come to a recognition of the inevitability of death. Then a dialogue between the caregiver and the person facing death can emerge, and the possibility for new responses can arise between them.

ও

When I was first dealing with my lymphoma, my husband told me he wanted me to be able to tell him everything I was feeling, no matter how crazy. I would wake him up in the middle of the night with bad dreams, or if I could not sleep, or if I was worried that they were going to cut off my leg because of one swollen lymph node. He held me, and I could go back to sleep. One day we were talking to friends about mutual truth telling in times of sickness or aging, and I realized that Charlie was not telling me his fears—he felt he needed to "protect me." This made me angry. Intimacy and caring were supposed to go only one way, according to him. No, I thought. I am a person of some strength and acceptance; I want to know what is going on with my husband. This was not a helpless patient he was living with. This was me. He was willing to some extent to do this. The opportunity for closeness between us was one of the beneficial side effects of the illness.

One day we talked about this inequality of self-exposure with a couple we're friends with, who are of different ages. Logan is eighty; Colette is close to sixty. Logan has urged her to tell him about her fears of losing him too soon in her life, but he "protects" her from his fears of dying. Colette reacted as I did, wanting to know more about Logan's feelings.

Colette had an emergency treatment for gallstones shortly after this conversation and nearly died. During that time, when the tables were turned, Logan began to talk to Colette about his fears of losing her unexpectedly. Colette was almost gleeful with this news when she spoke to me. This exchange offered the equality that she had wanted.

❧

Betsy, a massage therapist, had a business arrangement with Jim, who lived just a few miles away. For years, she gave him massages, and he did her taxes. Then he contracted multiple myeloma. She continued to care for him. Jim lived a long time with his cancer. His children were four and five when he was diagnosed, and by the time Betsy sensed that he was dying, the children were eleven and twelve. Jim had put up a good front for years and believed he would beat the odds. The family supported him in this approach, and he had indeed beaten the odds, but now he was dying. Betsy had spent a lot of time with people at the end of their lives, and by the quality of Jim's flesh, she knew the end was coming close. When she talked to Jim's wife about his decline, the wife asked Betsy to talk to Jim and tell him that the end of his life was near.

She did, and at first Jim was frightened. He was still hoping to get better. He said nothing to Betsy for the next two weeks when she visited him. Finally Betsy asked him how what she had said a few weeks earlier was sitting with him. Jim said he had been thinking about his death and wanted to say something to his loved ones, and he asked for Betsy's help. Jim had been a quiet, emotionally unexpressive person until his illness. Now he found himself wanting to speak about his feelings, but he was afraid he would not be able to express himself well. So Betsy suggested some things he might say to his children and his wife. "Tell them what is in your heart," was her advice.

Jim spoke to his children first and then turned to his wife. After she comforted him and complimented him on how open and caring he was with his children, he was able to use some of Betsy's suggestions:

I want you to know how much I love you and thank you for
   all these years together.
I know you have what it takes to raise our boys to manhood.
I know that you are equipped to deal with what comes.
I will miss you so much.
I will miss seeing the boys grow up.
I will miss being with you at the milestones in their lives and
   your life.
I will miss being by your side in old age.
I hope you will remarry.
I hope you will remember me, and remember me to our sons.
I hope you will remember the great times we have shared.
I hope you will find peace in your heart without me.
I love you.

Jim thanked Betsy so much for helping him to find the words.
With her help, he had been able to speak his piece to his wife and
children. He was relieved of his fears, and he began to surrender
his body to death.

≈

People are afraid to talk to each other about death, even when one
is dependent on the other financially as well as emotionally. Don
and Dawn came from Indiana to a residential program for people
with cancer. They had never talked about Don's possible death,
though he had a recurrence of a difficult cancer.

This week-long residential retreat is held in the rolling hills of rural western Maryland. The pond outside the retreat center is home to ducks, geese, fish, and deer. Early morning, as the participants stand at the window wall in the dining room waiting for morning yoga class to begin, they watch the mist rise off the water and the birds and animals that come down to the edge to drink. There are only eight or nine participants, one of whom may be a spouse or primary caregiver, and ten staff members. Yoga is offered twice a day. There is a morning support group each day, and there are discussions in the evenings regarding choices in cancer care. The afternoons are filled with individual meetings between participants and staff, art projects, walks in nature, and three massages. There are scheduled periods to talk about healing spaces, healing touch, nutrition, and creativity. The food is high-fiber, organic, vegetarian, and delicious.

On the third night of the retreat, there is a discussion about our beliefs, our fears, and our desires for care while dying as well as a more general exploration of what we know about death itself. People describe "good deaths" and "bad deaths." They describe their fears and hear those of other participants, which are often totally different. For many people this is their first opportunity to think about, feel, and talk about these subjects out loud. The tone of concerned appreciation for the enormity of the subject, its universality, and the comfort of the staff allow for exploration of these difficult subjects in a safe place.

Don and Dawn spoke briefly in the group and then went to their room and talked all night. What would she do? What did he want? How was each of them feeling? In the morning they reported this discussion, though not the content, to the staff. The retreat continued. At the end, on the way to the airport, I asked Dawn how the week had gone for her, the only caregiver in a group of eight people with cancer. She responded in a way that told me so much. She said, "After living with Don and his cancer for six years, I feel like I have just had a week off from cancer for the first time." Spending a week with people with cancer, exploring treatment options, nutrition questions, the use of yoga, massage, support groups, creative outlets, and mostly talking about the fears and possible death, allowed her to share the burdens of cancer and get on with living life as well. Talking about a difficult subject can shift it from an unmanageable load to a bearable reality.

&

A friend of thirty years calls me from St. Louis and says, "I look at my kids and I am so afraid I won't get to see them grow up." And she cries. Newly diagnosed with lung cancer, she cries when they are at school. I listen, and I wait. She will find her way back to words. Tears are cleansing. Speaking the fears out loud can be releasing. All I need to do is listen, I remind myself. She needs to experience her own sadness, her fear, and her ways to her strength. I might say, "It's so hard," or "I remember when I had a fear similar to that," or "It's okay to cry." Later, I might ask, "Do you have a safe place to cry these days?"

For parents with children at home, or anyone who continues to work, it is often very hard to find a time to mourn, to cry, a safe place to release the painful feelings. Some people feel they need to conceal their real feelings all the time. The small gasps of truth that can emerge in a phone call may be their only outlet and therefore terribly important. I try to listen and be with my friend. Facing dying with young children in the home is a wrenching situation, and there is no easy way through the pain. It is painful even to imagine for people who are not experiencing it. What we can offer to our friends is a gentle, neutral, listening ear and heart. There is no way to make it better, or to avoid it, or deny it. We can simply say, "I am so sorry."

ॐ

I was driving down to Washington, D.C., with my friend Brent after his prostate cancer was in remission, and he said that his greatest fear about dying was that he could not stand the idea of being dependent on others. He didn't want his family to have to clean up after him if he lost bowel control; he didn't want to give up driving, walking, or managing his own affairs. My greatest fear about the end of my life, I responded, was my fear of pain. But Brent was less concerned about this. He had had a lot of pain after his surgery and radiation, he told me. The pain had been un-expected, and it took some time before his doctor found the right pain relief. Brent learned from that experience that he could endure pain. He learned to meditate, to bring his awareness to the pain so it would sit a little farther from him. People visiting distracted him some, reading helped, laughing helped. He learned that the pain was never steady, but rather it ebbed and flowed. It was not unending. Sometimes it was hardly there. Eventually the pain ended. Now he knew he could get through it.

I listened closely. By taking in what Brent had said, I was able to find in myself the possibility of surmounting the pain as he had done. In turn, I talked to him about the pleasure of caring for my mother at the end of her life, how honored I was, and pleased to be able to give back to her. I hoped that Brent's children would feel that as well. To need physical care is a kind of dependence, but I had experienced my mother's need as a special gift to me. Helping her was an experience I cherish in my life. And Brent said he wondered if he too could embrace that perspective when he becomes dependent.

In the group setting, people try on each other's fears and loosen up about their own. Some people have fears that do not register for others. Some people are able to say, "What's so bad about losing bowel control? What's so bad about needing care twenty-four hours a day? Or about being seen looking bad?" Others feel deep sadness and fear about what will be missed, lost, unknown, the sadness that comes of not seeing their children grow, marry, and have children of their own. Overwhelming regret can lead people to wish for death, or for a lot more time. One woman, who had worked in a secretarial job for a company that produced faucets, wished she had some more time to offer her skills to a cause that made a difference in the world. She wanted to volunteer with children who needed to learn to read. The wish to leave a legacy can be a motivator for some people to give away money or share expertise before death. In hearing the fears and desires of others in a group, people report that their own fears shift. They find that learning that their fear is not universal, that there can be other responses to needing help, or that others wish they had spent more time caring for the planet helps them relax about their fears.

Some people report that by acknowledging their fear, by giving it time and attention rather than pushing it away, they loosen its stronghold on their psyche. If they greet the fear like an old friend, when fear arises, it becomes less threatening with time.

At a group I attended as a participant there was a go-round in which people told each other what they do to manage their fear. Some just need to describe the feeling out loud. Some need to find where the feeling resides in their body. They may explore the feeling in their body, even exaggerate it, feel it again and again, give it a color or texture or sound, and observe again how it feels. As the participants begin to explore their emotions in this way, to some extent they are taking control of them. If they can enlarge the fear, maybe they can reduce it. After locating the fear in the body, they may later be able to move it outside the body. Some people find it helpful to comfort themselves. "Of course this is painful." "Poor me. This is a big deal." "There, there." Saying, "I am so sorry this is happening to me," makes me feel better.

Turning to a positive visualization of an activity in a time of health may be the only way to get through a fear attack. If you acknowledge the fear and make a conscious choice to leave it for now and go somewhere pleasant, that control may relax the fear. I knew a woman who took herself mentally to a cottage in Maine when fear arose. She walked in the woods, sat on a log on the beach, all in her mind, and she was calmed.

Some people are able to recognize that fear is just another mind state, that it will not remain with them forever, that it is as fleeting as joy. As they move into this witnessing stance, fear releases its hold.

≥●

Anger and other dark feelings arise when a person faces illness, often with greater intensity than if there were no crisis. The inner experience of illness often makes people more emotional than usual but without any experience at expressing or working through the feelings. Each of us needs to find his or her own path to resolution. The following windows into people's lives illuminate different ways feelings about death and dying can motivate behaviors.

≥●

Diana, angry all her life, railed against the gods even up to her death. She was hard on her friends and demanding of her family. Anger was her currency. By the time Emila, the pastoral counselor, came into her life, Diana had driven most people away.

Emila is a quiet presence. Never flustered, she exudes neutrality and caring. Early in the relationship, she had to remind herself that what Diana said and did to her was just Diana's way. She realized that Diana used anger to protect herself from her fears of loneliness and death. Emila sat with Diana, held her hand and listened quietly, hoping that some of her calm and accepting manner would rub off on Diana. Even if it didn't, however, Emila was committed to staying with her until the end of Diana's life. She would care for her and show her acceptance even if Diana did not change.

Diana's belief that death would be terrible and that life was filled with suffering interfered with her ability to see what she was doing to limit her life. She would complain about the food that Emila brought. She would chastise her for coming late, or for coming at all, and then for leaving. Emila learned to open her heart to the neediness in Diana, not the outward behavior. She was accepting and patient. Over many months she experienced a slight softening in Diana when she was present. The attacks became fewer. Emila could discern that Diana was making an effort at control. Throughout it all, Emila continued to remind herself that the anger was not directed personally at her, but that Diana had treated people close to her this way her whole life. She felt Diana's underlying desire to be loved and her overriding need to test those who offered love. This knowledge was helpful to Emila in maintaining her equilibrium. Facing death did not make Diana soft and loving. Sometimes, even death cannot do that.

❧

Anne was angry about dying. That and only that aroused her rage. Anne had led a life of success and choice. She had succeeded in business and then left her business to follow her heart by working with disabled children. She had no children of her own, and this work of service was deeply fulfilling. After only two years in her new career, just as she was starting to feel competent, she was discovered to have an inoperable, fast-growing brain tumor. She was angry. Why was this happening when she had done everything to give meaning to her life? When she had followed her dream? When she had eaten an organic vegetarian diet for ten years? Why was this happening to her now? She wanted more time to work. She wanted enough time between treatments to feel strong enough to work with the children. She felt the staff at the school rejecting her need to return, since they did not want her to die on the job. Aside from her illness, Anne was a loving, excited, satisfied, engaging person. But her illness was now central to her existence. She was angry about that.

For Anne to find any kind of resolution for this anger, she needed to be able to talk it through repeatedly, until she became tired of hearing herself. She needed to find some acceptance in herself for being so angry. Anger was not a feeling that she had often allowed to surface before. All the repressed anger of Anne's life was contained in this final siege. Only when Anne recognized the validity of her rage, and its futility, was she able to move away from it. Later it arose again, but with less vigor, and what Anne found to replace the anger inside of her was hope: hope that she might find a way to enjoy every day in case it was her last day on earth. She began to think about drawing, singing, and gardening as perhaps less thrilling to her than the children, but a kinder way for her to live her last days than railing against the gods.

❧

When Katherine was diagnosed with colon cancer, she realized she had eaten badly at the trough of life for too long. She told her husband to leave. In order to heal she needed to be on her own. Her anger at her husband was poisoning her system. He had asked her to be understanding about the affairs he had, but she was tired of being understanding. She had given him space. She had tried to allow him to do what he wanted with his own body, but now she felt she had neither his body nor his heart. He left reluctantly. Throughout the final separation, the husband continued to parent their two children and help out at doctor appointments. She was relieved that she did not have to live with him and share a bed.

Katherine used her anger to leave her marriage. Now she could face her impending death free of this poisonous relationship. Her healing began when she told her husband to leave. She needed now to find people with whom she felt good, to be with her at the end of her life. Katherine had a few years on her own, feeling well, before the cancer came back. At the end, Katherine was surrounded by friends who loved and supported her.

❧

How much time we spend preparing for vacations! Buying tickets, making reservations and clothing lists, writing instructions on how to close the house, sending out our itinerary to relatives, changing the message on the answering machine, canceling the newspapers. And yet how much time do we give to planning for the longest journey of our lives, the journey into death? As we prepare for travel, job changes, moves, so too we need to prepare for dying. Many people find that the more they take care of the practical issues, the freer they are to live. Here are some kinds of preparation that can be carried out before death occurs:

Instructions for medical interventions at the end of life
Choosing a funeral home
Choosing a coffin and a cemetery plot
Purchasing burial insurance
Making funeral decisions: limousines, music, leader,
    speakers, clothes, religious rituals, and pallbearers
Finalizing a will
Reviewing the insurance coverage for health care, long-term
    care and death benefits

Even with all the planning in the world, sometimes the events of life take us away from our desires. Most people in America still die in hospitals. Many people die without the conscious knowledge that they are dying. Despite the attention that is beginning to be paid to pain relief, some people die in pain. Some, who would have preferred more time, die suddenly. Some die too young; some die more slowly than they would like. Planning needs to allow for the unexpected, without regrets and recrimination. Living wills, medical directives, conversations with loved ones and doctors are very important, but sometimes unexpected contingencies present themselves. It is useful to plan for a long, slow, gentle death, with the awareness that we can die in a moment. We can die in ways we never planned or wished for; much of the process is often out of our hands. Still, the planning allows for some sense of control and the opportunity to make our death as much the way we want it as possible.

❧

What is a good death? Dying can be scary, painful, noisy, distressing. It can also be peaceful, dreamy, uplifting. It takes strong intention and a team of caring, concerned people, both professionals and family, to make it more likely that death will be the latter. To shy away from death is to shy away from living. There are so many ways to die and so many moving stories from those who tend the dying that I become curious about my own death. What will it be like? What will I see? Feel? Do? I believe that if I dare to look at it, to plan as much as possible, I can make my death more like I want it to be than if I ignore the reality that I will die one day.

   Where do I want to die? On a mountaintop, in a chair, at home, on a beach, with flowers and songs, alone, with children? I can at least state my desires, and then, to the extent possible, I can try to create what I want. Visualizing what I want makes me feel hopeful. It seems more likely to happen.

❧

As a younger woman, Martha had been an advocate for social justice as well as a loving friend and relative to many people. Now, at ninety-eight, she was failing. She let it be known that she wanted to die at the beach. On hearing Martha's request, her granddaughter Nora called the hospital and had a stretcher delivered to her grandmother's house. She arranged for a great-grandson to come with his big open cargo van, and for Martha's niece, who was a caterer, to create a gourmet picnic. And off the family went to the beach below the Cliff House in San Francisco. The seals were lounging on the rocks that day, the June sunshine burned off the early morning fog, and with Martha stretched out comfortably among them, a great celebration of life took place. Three days later, Martha died, quietly, in her bed, at home.

❧

When Bill turned seventy, he threw a huge party at a hotel in downtown Cleveland. He invited friends from all parts of his life. He was already fighting colon cancer and wanted to celebrate being alive. People came from all over; one friend who had known Bill since childhood even arranged for a bagpiper to play late in the evening, since this was one of Bill's favorite musical instruments.

Less than a year later, Bill died. Again the bagpiper was called, and this time the music of the pipes accompanied Bill's casket to the grave site, followed by many of the people who had celebrated Bill's seventieth birthday with him.

❧

Tina was thirty-five the first time she was treated for breast cancer. Eighteen years later she developed another malignancy. Tina was in a new marriage and was experiencing a surge of creativity. This time, however, Tina knew that she would probably die. It was sooner than she had hoped, but she was at ease about it. She put her affairs in order and began to talk about what dying meant to her. She joined a group for women with metastasized breast cancer, where she could explore her feelings openly. She talked to her husband, a pediatrician. He was more frightened than she was, so Tina made sure she had a health-care proxy who could handle her decision making if necessary. She gave her husband a power of attorney to deal with her money, she updated her will, and she made funeral plans and wrote them all down. Then she felt calmer.

❧

Some things to consider about the dying process:

Do you want to be at home?
In hospice care?

In a hospital?

Do you want to be alone?

Surrounded by family and friends?

With a priest or rabbi?

Do you want extraordinary means for resuscitation?

As some specific point, do you want to be left free of medical
assistance?

Do you prefer to be pain-free and unconscious, or do you
prefer to tolerate some pain in order to maintain
consciousness?

Do you want to donate your organs?

Many deaths are not terribly painful. New methods of pain relief
are emerging all the time, and doctors, nurses, and hospice workers
receive training in this area. Some hospitals have departments
devoted to pain relief. It has been reassuring to me to know that
pain is not a given at the end of life, that morphine pumps,
epidurals, meditation, visualization, TENS machines, or biofeed-
back can transform death into an experience of acceptance, even
transcendence, for all involved.

&

Some people come to a point where they want to die. In a PBS
special by Bill Moyers on death and dying, one of the people he
followed kept pills in his drawer so he could choose when he would
die. But each day was not a day he wanted to die, until finally he

lost the physical ability to make that choice for himself, and he died when his time came. I believe that the period of time when he had the ability to choose was improved for him because he knew he had a way to end his life. He needed that reassurance.

Some people ask relatives to help them out of life. And then the relative has a very difficult choice to make: whether to fulfill that wish and live with the decision forever, or not to fulfill the wish and to live with that decision forever.

As a way to go gently into death, some people choose to stop eating and drinking at the end of life. Allowing a loved one to stop eating and drinking is extraordinarily hard for those who are present. It can be very difficult to witness and do nothing, but it can be a very gentle way to go.

Following people's health-care directives for their end-of-life care is an act of generosity. Making sure that hospital staff, nursing home staff, home health aides, and all family members attend to the stated wishes of the person can be the last chance to give of yourself to a person who is dying.

❧

Often the experience of facing death gives rise to a desire for reconciliation. As death approaches, it becomes more important to find forgiveness for ourselves and for those who have hurt us. When Tom lay dying, he realized that the person he most wanted with him was his estranged brother, Len. He and Len had not spoken for twenty years. The issue had been money; each felt victimized by the other. Over the years, relatives had tried to help heal the wounds, but the only progress was that the brothers could be in the same room together for large family events. Tom was in the hospital, connected to tubes, somewhat drugged, when images of their shared childhood began returning. He spoke to his wife about his desire to see Len—and his fears. He was afraid of being rebuffed; he was afraid he would not feel as forgiving in person. But he was also afraid of dying without seeing Len one more time. He came to realize that love and connection meant more to him than being right. He felt such love for the friends and family he had maintained relationships with all through his life, yet his own brother was not a part of this circle. He was angry with his brother for what had happened, but he wanted to love him anyway. It felt so messy to end his life without reaching out in some way. Victoria, his wife, called Len. She told him that Tom was asking for him and asked if he could please come. Len had been ready for years to make up, so he flew to Los Angeles to see his brother.

The brothers met alone in the hospital room. No wives or children were present. They never revealed how their conversation went, but, on leaving the room forty minutes later, Len said, "Thank God." After Tom's death, the families mourned together. The cousins began to visit each other after a separation of twenty years. Dara, Tom's younger daughter, told me that as a result of reconnecting with her cousins, aunt, and uncle, she had learned that withdrawing love is worse than any of the explicit issues in a controversy. Of course, one might ask, why wait until the very end of life to reconcile? Do it now.

❧

Ben flew to his father's bedside not knowing what to expect. He, his father, and his three brothers had not been in one place for seven years. Their father was critical and irascible. Ben was worried. He was tired of smoothing everything over. But this time he found his father in a different state. Ben's father asked forgiveness of each of his sons for his judgments, his distance, and his lack of love. The sons had never heard this from him before and hardly knew how to respond. It took time for them to begin to express to him their appreciation for what he had dared to do and to talk about what he had meant to them all their lives.

As his father talked, Ben was able to see his father in a new light. What he had always seen in his father as brusque and disaffirming he now saw as traits in himself that he had come to value. He called them tenacity, self-direction, and a discerning mind. Ben was not used to breaking through his own patterns of behavior. But with his father setting the stage, Ben rose to the occasion and told his father what he had meant to him. He called up memories of their good times together and turned old stories of victimhood around so they reflected the gifts the father had given him.

To reach a place of forgiveness takes work. Some steps to forgiveness might include

Reflecting on the intention of the other person in the act that
  caused the harm

Reflecting on your own intentions

Examining what you have derived from the story of blame
  and anger

Thinking about the price paid for being right

Considering the problem from the other person's side

Exploring what you value in relationships in general that
  may exist in this particular relationship

Evaluating what it would take to bridge the gap

Thinking of all the excuses you will use against asking for
  forgiveness

Recognizing that they are just excuses

Thinking of all the ways you will put off doing anything to
  change the situation

Finding a way back to wanting to bridge the gap

Imagining what asking for and giving forgiveness would feel
  like

Trying to reach out to the other person three times before
  giving up, and then trying again.

Sadly, it sometimes takes until the end of life for forgiveness and
reconciliation to take place. To accept an offer of reconciliation, or
a chance to forgive and be forgiven, is an unexpected gift of dying
that can mean so much to so many people. Not just the people who
have been estranged but also all those around them who have

longed for reconciliation for years reap the benefits of the coming together. We wish for well-being for strangers, for other species, for the planet, yet sometimes it is so hard to wish well those we once loved and now hold anger toward. Daring to say, "I'm sorry," is an essential step toward letting go.

એક

When Molly was dying, her friends took turns staying with her around the clock. While one slept in the waiting room, the other stayed in the hospital room with Molly. Molly did not speak for the last three days of her life, and each moment felt like it might be the last. Late one night, Molly's friend Kay was sleeping in the room with her. Every two minutes she lifted her head off the pillow to see if Molly was still breathing. So little of her seemed to be present in the room. It was late and dark. Kay checked and checked again, but finally she fell asleep. The next thing she knew, a nurse was in the room taking Molly's vital signs. Kay awoke to the nurse's presence and to her own clear recognition that Molly had died, that all was different. In those minutes while Kay was asleep, Molly had slipped away. Did she need Kay to be asleep to dare to leave? Kay asks herself this question. It was hard for Molly's friends to accept that after all the time they had spent at the hospital, no one was awake at the final moment. They must go on living knowing that perhaps being alone was what Molly needed to take her leave.

એક

As Wendy lay dying from lung cancer metastasized throughout her body, she tried to talk to her family about her death. They were still praying for miracles; they still wanted her to get better. Her family made plans for her recovery. Her biggest hurdle was her husband. He had never had the words for emotions. Each was protecting the other from the truth: He felt that she was giving up and was angry at her for it.

One day Wendy asked her daughter-in-law, Carrie, why the family seemed not to be aware that she, Wendy, was dying. Carrie told her that in the waiting room they all cried and cried together but didn't want her to see. They did not want her to take care of them, and they didn't want her to know that she was dying. This conversation was reassuring to Wendy, and she thanked Carrie for telling her the side of the story she could not see. Now she knew that her family knew that she was dying. She was relieved that she would not have to tell them.

At Wendy's next visit to her doctor, she spent some time asking about the dying process and confirming her awareness that she was indeed in the final days of her illness. This too comforted her. Her conversation with the doctor helped her tell her husband the truth. She let go of all her preconceptions of what he might say to her, and she spoke to him of her sadness at not living longer with him and her appreciation and love for him and all they had lived through. He returned her honesty and love and was able to tell her what she had meant to him. Then, one by one, she called into the room each of her children and their spouses and said her good-byes. Some of them were able to tell her what she had meant to them; others were not. But Wendy appeared calmed by these exchanges, and two days later she died.

Expressions of love and appreciation need not be paragraphs long. They may be three words: "I love you." The exchanges between spouses, lovers, friends, children, and parents may be very brief. They may take place in odd moments during the illness and be repeated from time to time. There are no rights and wrongs about how to do it. There is only the need to do or say something from the heart.

ख

When Adam was dying, he stopped eating and drinking and sank into a coma. The third day, which seemed like it might be one of his last, all his friends gathered in his sun-filled bedroom. His doctor was among them. Adam's doctor went up to him, shook him hard, and said, "Adam, all your friends are here to say good-bye. Wake up and be with them." Adam opened his eyes and looked at her. Then he pulled himself up into a sitting position and became more awake. For several hours that day he exchanged loving words and hugs with his friends and colleagues, then he sank back into unconsciousness and died the next day.

ख

Tuning in to what the person dying says is the best source of information. However, tuning in to the unspoken is important as well. As Evelyn lay dying, she said she hurt too much for anyone to touch her. Her grandson-in-law is a massage therapist. Almost without Evelyn's knowing it, he cupped her elbow gently in his hand, as she talked about the pain of endless blood drawing and needle insertions in her inner arm. Evelyn did not pull away. She left her arm cupped in his hand and began to relax. He did not stroke her; he just sent his warmth through the area of distress and into her heart.

Several people I know gave their parents massages as they lay dying, and afterward became certified massage therapists. The satisfaction they derived from the transmission of their love through touch made them want to do the same thing for others. A simple foot massage or hand massage may be a way to touch a person who is dying and dealing with pain. To touch near the point of pain is not acceptable. To run hands in the air, not touching the body but caressing the air around the body, can relieve tension and suffering, the psychological component of pain.

Getting into bed with a person who is dying may be the best way to be with him or her. This is only for a spouse or child or perhaps a very close friend. To lie quietly together, touching, holding, being, may be all that is needed.

Silence at the end of life can be better than talking. The good-byes have been said. The exchanges of feeling have been made. The effort to speak has become too much. The support of another being, present, silent, is a great gift.

Wetting the lips: When breathing becomes labored, when the fluids of the body are evaporating, when using the tongue to wet the lips is too much, it may be helpful to gently moisten the lips with a lip balm.

Playing tapes of loved ones' voices has been suggested by some families during the moments when no one is there. It's been reported that people in a coma may be able to hear. This might be a nice time for voices or music to be played in the room. There are tapes with birdcalls and the sounds of nature. Make a choice based on the person who is dying.

Candace told her health-care proxy that if she were ever to fall into a coma, the proxy should go out of the room if she needed to talk about difficult subjects with the doctor or friends.

Gentle reminiscences may pave the way to relaxation and ease for the one who is leaving. "Remember the time we stayed up all night singing show tunes." "Remember the restaurant we went to on Valentine's Day that we each secretly thought was too civilized." "Remember our trip with Elderhostel when the luggage took two days to turn up." "Remember the wind off Crete on the second day of the kayak trip."

Singing: As Margery lay dying, she reverted to the language of her childhood, French. Hour upon hour, her daughters sang to her old French lullabies that she had taught them. At first Margery joined in a little, but as the days passed and she no longer sang, she seemed to relax when her daughters began singing. Her breathing became softer, her movements easier.

Praying is not restricted to institutions and clerics. Prayer can take the form of any thought, wish, hope, belief, or statement of faith that feels good to the giver. It may be a psalm, prayer, or poem written by another; it may be a spontaneous experience in the moment. It can be said out loud or silently. Prayers can be surrounded by rituals. Lighting a candle for a loved one reminds us of that person. Saying daily morning or evening prayers for all of our sick friends works for some people. A kind thought in the course of the day, walking from the shop to the car, could be a prayer.

You can pray when you are with the person who is dying or when you are not with him. I had a hospital technician hold my hands in his and pray after he took my blood. He told me he was a minister, and I asked him to pray for me. I did not expect it to be so formal a prayer, but it felt good.

Releasing the body to death: There often comes a point when caregivers recognize that death is near, and that they are ready for their friend or loved one to die. The person who is dying can no longer go on as she has. Her quality of life left has been so reduced that she needs the ease of death. The struggle needs to end, so everyone will be released. At that point, putting these ideas into words can make a difference for the one who is suffering.

We will miss you, and we will be okay without you.
If you need to leave us, we understand.
It is okay to let go into death, whenever you need to.

May you find your way out of this life when you need to.
I see that you need to go; know that I will be all right.

Breathing practice: Sitting by the side of the bed, recognizing the
need for quiet and presence, I bring into my conscious mind the
rhythm of breathing of the person dying or suffering. I begin to
breathe with him. I bring my awareness to the breath and say to
myself: "Breathing in, I breathe in his pain. Breathing out, I
breathe calm."

There are many variations of this theme; making them up as I
sit with a person gives me a sense of purpose and calm. I am doing
something. I am not intruding. I am calming my friend and
myself.

Holding hands: To sit with a person who is dying and simply to
hold his or her hand, in silence, may be the best care possible for
the two of you. Hands get numb and lose their feeling after they
have been held for only a few minutes. Gently, quietly shift your
fingers when they need to be readjusted, for so do your partner's.

æ

As Marvin lay in the hospice facility at a hospital, dying from the
end stages of Alzheimer's disease, his daughter Sheila sat with
him. She hated to lose him, and she hated to see him struggling for
air. She came daily across the bay to San Francisco to be with him.
Again and again the nurses said he would not last the day, but he
lingered. One day Sheila's husband, Jacob, came with her. He

leaned over Marvin and told him how important he, Marvin, had been in his life. Then, clearly and strongly, he assured Marvin that he would take good care of Sheila. He loved her, he told Marvin, and would help her to mourn. Within the hour of Jacob's assertion, Marvin died.

❧

There are too many stories of people who arrive just a little too late and mourn those lost moments for years and years. One father arrived at the hospital after his middle-aged daughter had died. He went to the funeral home, where he sat with her body for hours, because he was not yet ready to say good-bye. Only after he had said everything that was in his heart and mind did he feel ready to leave her body. The funeral home staff respected his need and allowed him the time and privacy he wanted.

When Beth's parents died in a car crash, her greatest sorrow was that she was not with them as they died. Years later she was still talking about how hard it was to accept that they were truly dead, not having seen them dying. A psychiatrist suggested that she find a funeral with an open casket on the anniversary of their death and attend that funeral, look at the dead person, and have that person carry messages to her parents in heaven. Because Beth believed that souls went somewhere, she found that going to her parents' graves and addressing them, saying her good-byes and her thanks, and reviewing her memories of them in her head allowed her to begin to heal.

When I was unable to attend my grandmother's funeral because of a snowstorm, the same psychiatrist suggested I find a local funeral and go to it. Funerals are important rituals in the letting go into death.

I arrived at the hospital after my mother died. I was in the air on my way to her as she died. I hope she knew I was coming. I return to that thought over and over. I made sure to go to the funeral home and see her body, so I would know, truly, that she was dead. I had not believed that she was actually dying that week, though she was ninety years old and failing in many ways. I had been reading about death for several years and wanted so much to be with her, and yet I had not achieved that goal. She had wanted to die in a hospital, and she was ready to go—and she did. It was my need to be with her, not hers, but I was not, sadly. I stood with her body in the cold room, holding my nephew's hand and saying my silent prayers of good-bye, until I felt finished and ready to join the rest of the family in another room.

❧

There is no "wrong" way to mourn. Sometimes the differences between spouses in mourning are so large that one becomes angry with the other for not mourning his or her own way. Marriages can fall apart over this difference. Some people cry. Some can't. Some cry publicly and rend their garments. Others cry alone, under the covers. For some it takes years. We each need to find our way. I was at a funeral where the widow kept lamenting that it was her fault. She did not hear her husband's distress in the night, though she was sleeping next to him, and he died right there in bed beside her. People assured her she had not killed him, and still she cried. No one said to her, "It feels like you killed him. It feels awful to you that you let this happen. To wake up next to him and find him dead must have been terrible." No one acknowledged her internal pain. Yet to do so would have quieted her. If her relatives had honored her feelings and not simply corrected her, she might have forgiven herself more readily.

Win did believe in an afterlife and had a bet with a friend in my meditation group who was not a believer. He promised to try to send a sign. The night that Win died, there was a huge wind up and down the eastern seaboard. I remember commenting on it at our meditation group in New York City and hearing the windows rattling throughout meditation. The doubting friend had no doubt that night that Win had sent the wind to tell her, "There is more."

ॐ

Midge and Mike's older daughter died of a drug wrongfully given to her at the dentist's office, to which she was allergic. Midge cried earnestly and talked on the phone about her grief and her daughter. Mike barricaded himself in his workroom and would not talk. He stopped going to work, he stopped bowling, he stopped sleeping with Midge, and he stayed home. She kept talking about her grief. The more she talked, the quieter he became; the quieter he became, the more she talked. She wanted to go to grief counseling; he refused. She wanted him to hold her while she cried, but Mike feared that if he let go with Midge, he would never stop crying. He kept his silence and resented her for her way of mourning. Ultimately, they broke up. She was furious because she thought he didn't care about the child, or the loss, and that he no longer cared about her. He felt that she cared only about the child and not about him. They found no way to bridge the enormous and growing gulf. They had different ways of mourning and lacked the capacity to accept their differences.

What would have happened if they had talked about their different styles? If they had respected each other's style? Might it have been different if they had gone to a bereavement specialist? If they had had the wisdom and insight to recognize the pain each was in and allowed its different expressions? Or were there other insurmountable differences that only surfaced with this loss?

It is enough to say, "I am so sorry."

It is no help to say, "You will feel better soon."

It may be helpful to say, "You will remember him or her forever."

It is not helpful to say, "You will forget all this soon."

There is no need to say, "You can marry again, have another baby, or buy another dog."

"I'm so sorry" is enough.

Some other helpful things to say:

You are blessed with wonderful memories.
I will miss him or her too.
I am praying for a lessening in your pain.
I am praying that your wonderful courage carries you
    through this difficult time.
I am hopeful that you will find a way to go on living in the
    face of this sorrow.

᨞

When her son Donald died, Marlene was filled with every
emotion possible. From moment to moment she moved from
sadness, to loss, to relief, to anger, even to bouts of reluctant joy.
She wanted people to ask her about Donald and to speak of him,
but she did not want to be reminded of him, to answer questions,
to go back into the pain when she was having a moment of relief
from it. For months, there seemed to be no way anyone could get it
right: She always felt either ignored or intruded on.

Later she pondered the impossible conundrum she had imposed on her friends. How could someone have responded to
her that would have been comfortable for her? In a group with
other parents who had lost children, she discussed this very
common situation. What would be ideal, they finally decided, is
a simple statement that acknowledges the loss yet does not
demand engagement. For you as a friend or family member

simply to say, "I am thinking of . . ." in a neutral voice, lets the person who is mourning know you care yet does not demand any response. It just is. Respectful, quiet, brief, and useful in so many moments.

کم

Jenny was widowed in her early thirties. Happily remarried, a few years later she found she liked to be able to talk about Stuart, her late husband, naturally and easily, when conversing with old friends who knew him. She was different from Marlene in that she wanted to include Stuart in conversation. She noted that when she spoke of Stuart, her friends seized up and did not know what to do. She wanted to reassure them that it feels good to her to normalize his not being in this life anymore by including him in conversation. She thinks of him and likes to speak of him, as she would anyone they all knew.

کم

"I don't have to go to the cemetery to be near my mother. I can talk to her right here if I need to," a woman told me, sitting in the sun on a hilltop in Maryland. People who have lost a loved one vary widely in how they think of the departed. These stories may help you be neutral and accepting of everything that conversations with those in mourning reveal.

کم

Keeping an interested listening stance allows more of their thoughts and feelings to flow. A friend of mine who attended his father during his dying, and established an easy, loving relationship with him for the first time in their lives together, spoke to me of talking to his father after death. It was not the same for him with his mother. He and his mother had not had a troubled time in life, his work with her was done, and he reports he does not talk to her the way he often does with his father. The man who talked about these experiences is a college professor, intellectual, father, husband, and son.

A woman had a dream in which her dead mother came to her and told her she would be with the family at Easter and was sorry that the woman would be away in Arizona with her nuclear family, not with her siblings. Then the woman had to decide whether to visit with her family of origin or travel to Arizona with her children. Stories of people who receive unusual premonitions of the death of a loved one, though many miles away and not in technological connection, are fairly common. Roberta was studying in England and called home only once a month, on the last Sunday of the month. One night, very late, only a week after she had last spoken to her mother, Roberta had an uncontrollable need to call home. With difficulty, she found a phone booth and placed her call. While she was at a concert that night, her father had died suddenly of a heart attack. Roberta's beliefs were expanded by this experience, especially her beliefs about death being the end of everything.

Sharon entertained the possibility that there is some kind of existence after death on the earthly plane. Her father, a physicist, did not; nor did her mother. A year after her father died, on the anniversary of his death, that night, Sharon dreamed that he came to her and spoke to her. The exchange was comforting, though there was no concrete message. The next day, she decided to tell her mother about her dream. When she told her mother about her nighttime "visitor," her mother's response amazed her. "I dreamt of Daddy last night, too," she said, as though that were an ordinary event. As the two of them talked, they disclosed more parallels in their experience: The tone of the dream, the sweetness of it, and the lingering quality of the memory were all shared.

Knowing that the phone's ring is bringing bad news, knowing to call home at a most unlikely moment, hearing a voice, feeling a presence, having a dream in which the dead loved one appears at about the time of death are experiences that I hear about over and over when I facilitate conversations regarding death and dying.

After my father died, I felt his presence in my office for about a month. He had suffered from Alzheimer's disease at the end of his life, and he knew very little about my work at that time. It would have been of interest to him. I was developing housing for people who were mentally ill and homeless in New York City. My partner and I applied for renovation money from the city and state, purchased abandoned buildings, and created beautiful studio apartments. We selected service organizations to manage the buildings and support the tenants. My father was an engineer who designed buildings. He would have enjoyed looking at the blueprints and seeing the construction sites. For a month after his death, I introduced him to who I was and what I did in my office. This was a great surprise to me; this was my way of mourning.

These experiences of contact with loved ones across the divide of living and dying shape people's beliefs about an afterlife. By hearing the different ways the people in these stories hold death you will be more equipped to listen to yourself and your friends as you come to an understanding about their your own death.

ᴥ

As with illness, cards and e-mails are very welcome at the time of death. Even months later, if I learn someone I knew has died and he or she is on my mind, I will drop a note to the bereaved. Cards can be very brief. A short note of sympathy, or a remembrance, if you have a relevant anecdote or memory of the deceased, goes far in comforting the mourners. People know how hard it is to write and send a card. You can say

I am thinking of you at this time.
I am remembering my experiences with _____ and
     treasuring those moments.
I send you my good wishes to support you through this
     difficult time.
The world is a richer place for _____ having been here.
May you find your way to some peace with your loss.

When six of us could not be at our friend Melissa's memorial service, we made a date and gathered at a meditation room in the hospital. With no plan beforehand, just our own personal need at that moment, we created a service that included poetry readings, a cluster of rose petals, scented candles, personal prayers, and an exchange of memories. Leaving there with Melissa's memory wafting around us, we felt the relief that comes through a communal grieving process.

❧

Two months after Jessica died, and during the week of her birthday, her son Glen was married at the family home. High on a hill surrounded by mountains and sunlight, flowers and friends, the family gathered again, this time to celebrate. Most of the guests knew that Jessica had just died, and all wanted to honor the joy of the day. Her husband, Francis, needed a way to include Jessica in the day. He placed her favorite white Adirondack chair just up the hill, above the wedding ceremony, under a live oak tree, on the spot where Jessica had placed the chair and sat all afternoon when she received her diagnosis. The empty chair provided a place for the celebrants' thoughts and love for Jessica. It gave Francis a way to feel she was with him, celebrating the marriage of their son.

7. Final Thoughts:
Let Compassion Guide Your Heart

Embracing both joy and sorrow
Our heart can remain
Tender and wise
            —Jack Kornfield

THOUGHTS FOR THE GIVER

Compassion occurs when we open our feelings to the feelings of another person, without judgement, pity, or a need to fix. It is an act of holding the fullness of feelings of another in our awareness and feeling suffering or joy with him or her; without becoming lost in the feeling.

As our hearts open to another, as our desire to respond to another person's suffering arises, the question is: what to do to express these desires? When the underlying intentions include awareness, careful listening, and speaking from the heart, the resultant words or deeds will be right. And they will touch the heart of the receiver.

❧

Sensitivity increases in the face of illness. When illness enters the picture, loved ones want even more than usual to "get it right." The person who is ill wants more than ever to have it her way. She may feel she is handling all she can; this is not a time to have to correct loved ones. While the caregiver wants to please, he may be so immersed in his own feelings that it is hard to put himself in the place of the sick one.

&

Do something when you feel the urge. A brief telephone call or greeting card means a great deal to a person who is sick. The sense of being held in a cocoon of love and prayers was as important as medical treatments to me during my stem cell transplant. Just a note or e-mail that says, "Thinking of you," is all it takes. A note written months later, "Sorry it took me so long. I have been thinking of you," can relieve the sender and touch the friend.

&

Speak from the heart. The words can be simple and heartfelt. "I miss you," "I hope you feel better soon," or "I wish I were there with you." Some people are more articulate, sometimes funny, even eloquent, but each expression of concern that reflects that person is perfect in itself as it stands and is all that is needed. A pure statement of what you are feeling is always right.

&

The relationship determines the kind of interaction. The duration, connection, and love in the relationship determine what follows. If you have always cared for someone who is now ill, you will continue to care for that person, perhaps even more so. If it is a parent who is ill, it may be your turn to give back. If it is a friend, you need to evaluate carefully what the relationship was like before illness entered the picture. With awareness as to what you can offer easily, and how many other people are helping as well, the giver can ask, "What can I do?" And then listen carefully to the response. Let the wishes of the person who is ill be the guide, not your agenda. Over time, a person who is ill has changing needs and the ability to accept help changes. From time to time, ask the question, "What can I do?" again.

❧

Deep, quiet listening is a great gift. Whether it is a doctor, a daughter, a mother, or a lover, no matter how well the attending person thinks she knows the person who is sick, she will learn even more by asking open-ended questions and then listening. The doctors in an earlier chapter had to listen very closely to their patients in order to respond to them as well as they did.

Sometimes when people are ill, those who are caring for them need to listen to the sick person's silences as well as his words. Silence may mean dissent. Respecting a person's need to have as much independent functioning as possible requires careful listening.

There are times I think I know what should be done for someone else. I want to fix and give, solve and make better as fast as possible. But that is for my own sake, not for the sake of the receiver. Sometimes, for the person who is sick, the gift of time—time to arrive at a decision, time to find the right practitioner, time to be sad, fearful, anxious—is most valuable in finding her way back to hope and health. Allowing the unfolding of the individual journey, being present with a friend or relative, letting her know that I support whatever she chooses, that is the gift.

Thinking that we know what is right for other people is not respectful of their autonomy, their right to live their life as they choose. Simply to listen, to nod, to agree, to accept—this is respect.

There will be differences of opinion. Family members are deeply affected by the illness of one of their members, and they won't always agree. It may be parents and an adult child who clash, it may be sisters, spouses, or partners. Anyone in these close relationships may find himself or herself in conflict. And when it occurs around illness, the disagreement will be intensified by the importance of the moment and the issues. All parties may feel they are absolutely right. But this is no time for power struggles. This is when the best in each must come forth, and when understanding, listening, and caring are necessary to arrive at a solution that allows for everyone's various needs, with particular attention and weight given to the one who is ill. We need to explore what underlies the various options—what reasons exist, what possible drawbacks, and what potential good results. What are the hopes, the desires, the pain, the fears that underlie the issue? Only then can choices be made that are acceptable to all parties.

Dealing with illness calls up hard feelings for caregivers. Caregivers may have anger and fear and sadness to deal with. Where or with whom is it safe for caregivers to let out the pain they are carrying? They do not want to burden their loved one who is sick. They may be unaccustomed to releasing, or talking through, or even recognizing their feelings. They may feel guilty for having negative feelings. And yet the feelings are there. Caregivers need caring friends at this time too, friends who have experienced some of what is happening and can ask the questions that lead to a conversation. The issues might include how hard it is to be a caregiver, the fear of not being able to do the job, the fear of ultimately losing the loved one, the anger at some behaviors or decisions, the need to be recognized, or alone, or sad—all these need a place to be explored.

Feedback is part of caring. If there are warm feelings on both sides, all you need to do as a friend is ask, do, and then ask if what you did was helpful. If communications have been open and easy before illness entered, they can remain easy in the face of illness. Thinking about what I would want if I were on the receiving end is often a useful guide for my actions. It is easy enough to ask, "Does this work for you? Please tell me if I could do this better." Given the sensitivity around what to do and say, unless the person who is ill speaks out loud with specificity and care about what pleases him or her, no one will ever know.

Find a balance between doing too much and doing nothing. There are two sides to the coin of helping and not helping. Extremes on either side can cause difficulty. There are people who want to do too much, people who find it hard to listen to the desires for independence of the person who is ill. Caregivers who are too present and too helpful can undermine the self-determination of the person who is sick. This can be as hard to deal with as people who disappear when illness or disabilities appear.

If at first you don't succeed, try, try again. So many people have felt they have made mistakes in their response to illness. Don't put off apologies; life can be too short. Reopen the subject and try again. The friendship between you will usually allow forgiveness to flow. What you are uncomfortable about saying may not even have registered with the receiver. It is a sign of caring to want to make your words better.

Ask if they want you to ask. People with chronic illness need attention too. Just because the malady is for an extended period does not mean that the person doesn't want her struggle to be acknowledged. However, with chronic illness, there are more years to get tired of answering the same questions over and over, and so when you offer your sympathy you have to learn what your friend wants you to ask. With respect, you need to inquire into what she wants on a particular day and, from her responses over time, shade and shape your comments to suit her desires. Take care and time. Your interest and respect will be appreciated. Some like attention;

others hate it. Some vary day to day. You need to find out what your friend's wishes are.

Statements are a very kind way to show concern. Sometimes, when you see a person who you know is dealing with illness or a significant loss, rather than asking him questions about the painful subject, you can make a statement: "I am thinking about your situation." It gives him the space to be silent, or to fill you in if there has been a change. And it gives you a chance to express your concern without any response being demanded in return.

With sadness, just be there. Sadness can give rise to tears. All you need to do when a friend cries is be with her. Touch her if you are comfortable doing so. If that is not something you do, just to be present is enough. Some people cry easily and long. For others it is an occasional event and hard to reach. Many people tear up, and that is as far as it goes. It can be a great release to cry. If you stay quietly present, your tears will run their course. Do not fear. They never go on forever. Tears wash the soul. They cleanse the heart. Unshed tears can hurt. What a moment of love it was for me to cry with my friend recently on a bench in Riverside Park. Who was crying for whom, or what, did not matter. We were, in that moment, two women feeling sadness—and expressing it.

≥

Don't forget to give compliments. Sincere compliments are often appreciated. Finding the words to compliment some real aspect of the person who is dealing with illness gives great energy to the receiver. These moments of contact that reinforce health—moments of laughter, smiling, joking, flirting, and complimenting—all bring the sick person back into the world of the well.

ð

Be kind toward yourself and others. Kindness can be a choice for the person who is ill, as well as the caregiver. To the greatest extent you are each able, act from kindness every day. Do I want to leave a legacy of anxiety, discontent, and anger—or of kindness? Moments of appreciation for the smallest of attentions can create an atmosphere in which more kindness arises. Some days it is hard to find anything but despair. Connecting with the sense of being part of something larger than yourself, part of a universe of suffering and healing, is a way back into kindness for yourself and others. Sometimes we blame ourselves for not feeling stronger, or happier, or smarter. Pausing to note that the voice with which we talk to ourselves is harsher than the voice we use with anyone else can make us aware of our self-condemnation. This is no way to treat a sick person. Leave yourself alone. Treat yourself kindly.

Speak from the heart. Many people who have dealt with a challenging illness report an experience of strength and clarity. There comes a realization, more than ever before, that if you do not say or do what is true for you now, you are undermining your very life. People become bolder, clearer, more aware of their needs, and more willing to ask for what they want, nicely. This is not about being demanding. It is about recognizing one's own value to self and others.

Conversations about illness, dying, death, funerals, mourning, remembering, and finally letting go are very important in friendships and within families. The ways we talk about illness and death are dependent on the age and relationship of the listener. To dare to talk about the end-of-life issues usually enhances the relationship of the listener and talker and allows each to live more fully until death comes. It is a parent's job to introduce children to this side of life. Introducing children to death so that it is a part of life, giving them an understanding that we are all mortal, is essential. It's helpful for this to happen before illness or death comes into the family.

❧

Think about mending fences. During illness, when people realize their mortality, they may want to reconnect with relatives or friends from whom they have become estranged. Putting reconciliation off makes it harder. If there is an impulse in the face of illness or death to bridge the gap, it is worth stepping into the space and trying.

Learn the gift of receiving. One of the occasions for growth when a person is sick is learning to receive. Sometimes this is the hardest lesson of all: just to say, "Thank you." It may help to remind yourself that you would do the same for another if he or she needed similar assistance. Recognize the joy it gives to the giver to be able to be helpful. Sometimes we give back to those who helped us; sometimes we give aid to the next person in our life who needs it. There is enough love to go around.

ॐ

Find an outlet for hard feelings. Even more than in health, there are many layers and moment-to-moment changes in the emotional state of the person who is sick. There need to be outlets for those feelings—to help them to arise and to pass. Sometimes merely naming them internally can release them. Sometimes they need to be talked about over and over. Sometimes a cry is needed. Thinking about where and with whom the expression of feelings can best take place is a kindness to all concerned.

ॐ

Doctors are people too. Doctor/patient relationships are more difficult than relationships with friends. The expectations are higher; the disappointments are greater. Remembering to ask for what you want, and expressing what you feel from time to time, can draw a great deal of humanity from your doctor. Doctors are in the profession because they are people who care about other people. Sometimes that gets lost, and sometimes it shines forth. Sometimes you can help your doctors let this impulse shine forth in a supportive and healing way.

ॐ

With compassion, attention to the relationship, self-awareness, and love, your ways of relating to others in time of need can be made smooth. The acts of giving and receiving bring joy to all parties. After reading the stories of the people in this book, I hope your increased awareness will make this give-and-take easier and freer.

Postscript

I sat down to write this postscript in the spring of 2003, after a break of a few months during which I had a stem cell transplant, with the hope of curing my lymphoma. My quiet, polite, slow-growing lymphoma had transformed into a fast, aggressive lymphoma, and it was time to treat it aggressively. It was just two years since I had last received chemotherapy, and I was reluctant to give up feeling healthy again so soon. I spoke to many doctors to see if there were other treatments that would offer me as likely a cure as the transplant. I carried in my head many images of friends who had been terribly sick during their transplant process. The stories of debilitation and pain were dire, though all are alive today. I already had some loss of feeling in my toes and one leg that was bigger than the other from accumulated lymph fluid that wasn't draining—and that was all I could handle. I like to hike and kayak, sit on the floor with my grandchildren, and bounce up each day with good energy. I had all that before the transplant, and I would have to give up a great deal of good energy for several months as well as having a few more residual side effects at the end.

The treatment consists of three days of high-dose chemotherapy, followed by a few hours of having my own previously harvested and frozen stem cells put back into my body. Then all I had to do was stay in my hospital room for fourteen days, keep away from germs, take all the pills and solutions they had prescribed to protect me from side effects, and get well. That was it. I was fed, visited, tested, weighed, and cared for in every way possible.

What happened for me was so much better than I ever expected that I experienced a kind of ecstasy from time to time in the hospital and on first returning home. Each day I could sit up in hospital bed, slide on my black clogs, grab my IV pole in my right hand, and walk, upright, jauntily, and as easily as ever, over to the bathroom about ten steps away. The ability to feel rather like myself one day after the transplant, two, then three days after, was so reassuring, so surprising, that my heart sang inside of me. Each moment of feeling all right was precious.

Day after day, different friends and family members came to see me. Day after day, in an intensified form, I was able to experience the gift of giving and the gift of receiving, which I had been writing about with some knowledge. But this knowledge was now highlighted by being inside the exchange yet again. The joy came from surviving well because of the care and love of those with me and those who sent their cheers from far away.

The periods of intense joy grew out of finding that my body was going to get through this. I found that even on days when my body was not as strong as usual, or on days when I can a fever or had some reaction to a drug, I could still be in reasonable spirits. That my happiness did not depend on my health was new to me. Most important was the support and care I received from everyone I knew, including my new friends, the hospital staff. The experience of being held on a cloud of love, knowing that I did not have to do this work alone, that I could release myself into the sustaining arms of others—if only symbolic—made it possible for me to lie in the bed and heal. I did not have to will myself well. I did not have to fix or do anything. I could receive, and that was fulfilling for others, and new for me. To sense in myself that I would be okay. That whatever happened, I would be okay.

The intense joy came also from the personal work I did to maintain my center and my calm. When I found myself uncomfortable, I would take three deep breaths and gently breathe them out. I would look at the ceiling and remind myself that this too would pass. My ability to make some choices about attitude, being present in the moment, and connection with others were enough to sustain me day to day in the slow process of the recovery. That my methods of finding my strength worked energized me and gave me comfort. These unexpected abilities added to the sense of joy and personal power that was flowing in the room.

A great lesson was that of the reciprocity of giving and receiving. I would lie in bed. My husband was not able to be with me all day, though sometimes he came three times in one day, so he arranged a schedule of friends to spend a few hours with me when he was not there. Each day the door opened, and in came a dear person in my life. Each came in, somewhat unsure of how I would be, how they would be, what to do or say. And each time my pleasure in their arrival and their pleasure at being there was conveyed between us, lifting them and me up into a place of ease and connection and delight. We would talk for a while, then I would grow sleepy and roll over to go to sleep. Often people stayed. Sometimes I needed some time alone. At first it was hard to go to sleep with people in the room, but I learned how. Sometimes they slept too. But what I realized is what an intense, unusual exchange takes place in the hospital room. It meant so much to me to have people come. Each person, just by accepting me however I was at the moment, lifted me to a better place. I moved into a reality where my momentary discomforts did not need recognition. Instead, love was the unstated undercurrent. I would never have wanted any of my visitors to do anything different from what they did. They were all utterly true to themselves—giving to me, probably very aware of how they were with me, listening, responding, asking, and caring. I in turn tried to give them feedback that what they were doing was perfect for me and meant so much to me.

I tell this to underline the importance of being there, doing something. It is hard to go wrong. When people are in a vulnerable state there is a good chance that they will appreciate your acts of kindness. You do not have to be fearful. You were friends before; you liked each other before; you can still be friends as easily as you were.

Every week my husband sent out an e-mail to people we know, and each day he received responses. His favorite activity was printing these out and reading them to me. For both of us these notes and letters were a source of endless sustenance. They reminded us of our strengths in dealing with this situation, they reminded us of easier times, they added to the feeling of being supported on love. We were not alone in a hospital on Ashby Avenue in Berkeley, California, doing something very difficult; we were together, surrounded by the prayers of people we know all over the planet who wanted it all to go well and easily for me. And it made a huge difference. Whether the notes just said, "Thinking of you," or were longer—funny, literate, unexpected—they all played their part in the healing process.

I gave a gift when I invited people into the inner sanctum, and they gave me a gift by coming. I delighted in the conversation, whatever it was—different every time, each person's unique energy entering my room and bringing with it smiles and laughter, acceptance of whatever mood I was in, and encouragement.

Opening the heart as a receiver of love and care makes exchange equal. It is not all one person giving, one receiving. It is the reciprocity of giving and receiving that gives rise to joy.

Acknowledgments

The Etiquette of Illness grew out of four weeks in residence at the Rockefeller Foundation Scholars Program, in Bellagio, Italy, in the spring of 2001. The quiet and the scholarly work around me inspired this undertaking.

I am grateful to Jane Anne Staw, whose enthusiasm for the project kept me working. She gave me deadlines, helped me to believe in my book, and quietly led me see what was missing.

I thank Paul Gorman for the original idea of writing on this subject.

The book relies on my interactions with many people. I am grateful to all of them for all that they taught me. To the people whose experiences illuminate the pages of this book, I thank you for your willingness to share your perspectives with me.

My children and husband have supported and encouraged me. To my friends and family who are and are not in the book, I thank you for your belief that I could do this.

I thank my agent, Janis Donnaud, for her appreciative and enthusiastic response to the manuscript. I thank Bloomsbury, especially my editor Amanda Katz, for her careful reading. Thanks go to Karen Rinaldi, also of Bloomsbury, who liked my book and who called me two days before I began chemotherapy and offered to publish it. The promise of having the book come out carried me through treatment and recovery.

My deepest thanks to my husband, Charlie, whose care for me and support all these years made this book come to fruition.

A NOTE ON THE AUTHOR

Susan P. Halpern is a social worker and
psychotherapist. She is the founder of the New
York Cancer Help program and a staff associate at
the Commonweal Cancer Help Program. She
lives with her husband, near their children and
grandchildren in Berkeley, California.

A NOTE ON THE TYPE

The text of this book is set in Adobe Caslon,
named after the English punch-cutter and type-
founder William Caslon I (1692–1766). Caslon's
rather old-fashioned types were modeled on
seventeenth-century Dutch designs, but found
wide acceptance throughout the English-
speaking world for much of the eighteenth century until being replaced by newer types toward
the end of the century. Used in 1776 to print the
Declaration of Independence, they were revived
in the nineteenth century and have been popular
ever since, particularly among fine printers.
There are several digital versions, of which Carol
Twombly's Adobe Caslon is one.